THE RESILIENT SHINAI
— A HISTORY OF KENDO IN CANADA —

Hirokazu Okusa

First edition published in June 2023
Bunkasha International Corporation
2498-8 Oyumicho, Chuo-ku, Chiba-shi, Chiba, Japan

Written by Hirokazu Okusa
Editorial supervision by Alexander Bennett, Michael Ishimatsu-Prime
Design and Layout by Bunkasha International Corporation

ISBN: 978-4-907009-37-3

Messages

Former President, International Kendo Federation

Fujio Cho

This book is a detailed account of the history of the spread of kendo in Canada. It will surely be of interest not only to actual practitioners, but also to those even with only a general interest in kendo.

As mentioned in this book, Mr. Hirokazu Okusa has not only made great efforts to develop and spread kendo as a former president of the Canadian Kendo Federation, but he has also contributed to its dissemination around the World as a former director of the International Kendo Federation. Based on his experiences he wanted to document how kendo, a traditional Japanese martial art, spread in North America, especially in Canada. He shows how kendo became an important part of the lives of Japanese-Canadians and Canadians in general. As such, this volume will serve as a tremendously useful resource.

In 2020, the International Kendo Federation, which was founded in 1970, celebrated its 50th anniversary. Chapter Four discusses the efforts of Torao Mori. He was the first president of the Kendo Federation of the USA and a central figure working towards the establishment of the International Kendo Federation and the World Kendo Championships. He passed away one year before these monumental developments in modern kendo were realized. Seventeen countries and regions including Japan, Canada, and the USA came together to form the International Kendo Federation. Now, 50 years later, the federation has continued to grow and has 59 affiliates. I am always deeply impressed when I see so many international kendo practitioners training hard in their chosen art.

Chapter Four contains a description of the strength and dynamism of Torao Mori's kendo. I found the name of Junichi Haga-sensei, a great master who taught me when I was a student. It brought back many fond memories.

Kendo, begins and ends with courtesy. The purpose is not only to compete and win against opponents with superior technique but is based on a philosophy of "polishing the mind, strengthening the body, and aiming for development of one's character." This idea has its roots in the time-honored spiritual culture of Japan. I believe that kendo has spread successfully around the world because it contains universal wisdom. Throughout this book, it is clear that the pioneers of kendo in Canada continued to practice in the face of great adversity and worked tirelessly popularize it there.

I would like to express my sincere respect to those people. I also hope that kendo enthusiasts around the world continue to develop mutual trust and friendship through kendo.

Former President, Canadian Kendo Fédération

Dr. Christian D'Orangeville

At the 17th Canadian National Kendo Championship held in Vancouver, BC, in 2011, the Canadian Kendo Federation celebrated 100 years of kendo in Canada - an impressive milestone.

To know the history of the early Japanese immigrants landing on Canada's west coast in the late 1800s, is a kind of moral obligation for anyone holding a *shinai* in a Canadian dojo today. The handful of early Canadian kendo pioneers gave a precious heritage to future generations, and to all Canadians, imparting their knowledge and passion for kendo. These were men with a destiny. This may explain, to some degree, the strength and vitality of Canadian kendo today, both as a strict martial art and as an instrument of soft multiculturalism.

This book's author, Mr. Hirokazu Okusa, former CKF President, had a successful career as a talented Japanese gardener and businessman, but he always carried in his heart a passion for our martial arts and his native Japanese culture. I remember Okusa-sensei many years ago, training alone without any rest in his personal dojo, Zosokan, built in the middle of his rural property in a suburb of Vancouver.

All kendo practitioners in Canada and abroad should be thankful to Mr. Okusa for his tireless efforts in completing this first historical study *The Resilient Shinai*, not as a professional historian, but as a passionate and cultivated Canadian man who was born in Japan but set down roots here. He traces the struggles of these resilient Japanese-born men and their passion for kendo, honouring the art's Japanese roots and budo spirit; a heritage and passion that holds strong, even in dark times.

I wish this important document a long journey!

The Bulletin: a journal of Japanese Canadian community, history & culture

John Endo Greenaway

Managing Editor

To read *The Resilient Shinai, a History of Canadian Kendo* is to gain an appreciation of the resilience of the early Japanese immigrants who settled in Canada at the turn of the twentieth century. The spirit of *gaman* and *ganbatte* – fortitude and perseverance – is embodied in the early kendo pioneers who are documented in this carefully assembled book.

Hirokazu Okusa, himself an immigrant to Canada and one-time president of the Canadian Kendo Federation, has spent years researching and documenting the history of kendo in Canada. He painstakingly traces its growth, from the Japanese immigrant communities throughout British Columbia, through its survival during the World War II internment, to its transformation after the war, when it spread out across Canada, following the movement of the community east.

With most professions barred to them, many of the early kendo practitioners were fishermen, farmers, foresters, and millworkers. Okusa paints a vivid portrait of a community in transition, documenting the establishment and growth of the various kendo dojos and tournaments as Japanese Canadian communities grew and prospered on the west coast, well-illustrated by many historical photos.

With an entire chapter devoted to the wartime nurturing of kendo, particularly in the Angler POW camp on the shores of Ontario's Lake Superior, Okusa makes the case that kendo in Canada is unique among countries where kendo has taken root. The dedication shown by the Shoko *kenshi*, who fashioned their own *shinai* (swords) from strips of birch in place of the traditional bamboo, has clearly been an inspiration to the author in his own dedication to the art of kendo, transplanted to his new homeland.

In documenting the numerous kendo clubs that sprang up across the country following the loosening of wartime restrictions, Okusa shows how the influence and leadership of the early kendo pioneers gradually gave way to a new wave of young leaders, first from Japan and then increasingly from other countries, mirroring the increased popularity of kendo around the globe.

Non-kendo people will find much to value here. In carefully crafting this comprehensive record of kendo in Canada, Hirokazu Okusa adds another important chapter to the accumulated history of the Japanese Canadian community, in all its many permutations.

Alex Bennett
Professor, Kansai University

Bamboo

Zen Buddhism provides us with wonderful sayings that convey the essence of the human mind and experience. One phrase that I like in particular is "*Take joge no fushi ari*" (竹有上下節) which I render into English as "Bamboo has upper and lower nodes…" This Zen phrase has many meanings and interpretations, and the fact that it is about bamboo makes it even more germane to kendo people.

It literally means that just as there are upper and lower nodes in bamboo, there are also distinctions among people, and that no matter how well people get along, each has his or her own position and way of thinking. Furthermore, social harmony cannot be maintained unless courtesy and moderation are observed. This is a fundamental idea in society at large, and something that we think about a lot in the dojo as we engage in combat with all manner of kenshi.

Bamboo is a fascinating plant. The space between the nodes is hollow, but the joints themselves are rigid and unyielding. Bamboo maintains its flexibility and strength by striking a balance between the stiffness of the joints and the malleability of the hollow space in the internodes. In the context of the Zen phrase, our daily life is represented by the hollow internodes. In contrast, various events such as anniversaries and other important milestones are the knotty parts.

If we just go through the motions in our daily lives, our hearts and bodies will break someday. Therefore, just as with bamboo, the role of nodes is important for both organizations and individuals. By creating and celebrating milestones, we are able to recognize the past, look to the future, and take a fresh look at the present. This allows us to make sense of our current circumstances, and take appropriate action to respond to adversity, just as the pliant bamboo plant rolls graciously when battered by strong winds in a storm. This is the resilient *shinai*.

This wonderful book by Okusa-sensei represents a node in the history of Canadian kendo. It is a milestone in and of itself that serves to chronicle all of the other milestones, and trials and tribulations experienced by generations of kenshi who nurtured kendo in Canada. Congratulations on a life dedicated to the promotion of kendo, Okusa-sensei. This volume is a monumental contribution and a guide to us all. This Haiku always reminds me of you.

Bamboo canes knocking   Maple leaves all aflutter   Wind out of the east

CONTENTS

PREFACE

In 2011, during the Canadian National Kendo Championships in Vancouver, British Columbia, the Canadian Kendo Federation (CKF) celebrated the Centenary of kendo in Canada. As part of the celebration the CKF established a historical committee to collect historical material and published *Kendo in Canada to 1946*. This booklet was edited and published with great effort by Professor Emeritus of History B. Wakabayashi of York University, Ontario. Also, during my visit to Mr. Katashi Hibi in Thunder Bay, Ontario, on the occasion of presenting him with the "Canadian Kendo Federation Award of Appreciation" as a pioneer of kendo in Canada, he presented me with a copy of his book *Dawning of Pine Lake*. Mr. Hibi was a manager of Shoko Dojo at Angler, a camp which will be discussed in a following chapter. These two events ignited my spirit to attempt a book on the history of kendo in Canada. I felt it was important that a record is kept of our daily martial life. As a historical record in four chapters, I am aware that it is impossible to cover everything completely and accurately. I would like to express my apologies for any mistakes or omissions that may be present.

For this project, many people contributed historical materials while others allowed me to interview them. I would like to thank the following people for their time and valuable information: (Angler) Katashi Hibi, Shigeru Kuwabara; (Kaslo) Susumu Tabata; (Ocean Falls) George Takahara; (Raymond) Kuni Ikuta, Teruko Ikuta, Roy Akune, Ted Koyata; and (Steveston) Toshio Murao, Fumi Hayashi, Shizu Hayashi, and Jim Murray. Also thank you to Bryan Asa, Christian D'Orangeville, Ray Murao, Mark Noda, Morito Tsumura, Gilles Valiquette, and Tom Yamashita for their valuable information and suggestions.

This book is based on the articles I wrote for the Japanese kendo magazine *Kendo Nippon*, editor Mr. Yuichiro Ando. Thank you to the author, Toshiyuki Hayase for the book *The Man Called Tiger Mori* published by Ski Journal , 1991. I especially would like to thank Hirotaka Ara-sensei who passed on to me Rintaro Hayashi-sensei's private collection of writings, memos and photos. I am glad to use this precious historical information that Rintaro Hayashi left us. Without this material, I would not be able to write about Canadian kendo history in the pre-war period. I am glad to introduce these past figures who are totally forgotten among our kendo friends nowadays.

I would like to thank the following people and organizations for their assistance in putting this book together: Masaki Watanabe who translated my Japanese articles into English as a starting point for this book; Moe Ezaki, John Endo Greenaway and David Chiu for proofreading and editing; Linda Reid and Lisa Uyeda for their professional archival assistance; and the Nikkei National Museum and Cultural Centre Library and Archives Canada for the wonderful photos.

Also thank you to Michael Ishimatsu-Prime, Alex Bennett, Mako Inouye, and Yulin Zhuang at Bunkasha International for editing and proofreading.

Finally, thank you to the National Association of Japanese Canadians for the project grant that enabled this book to be published.

INTRODUCTION

In kendo, life is expressed by a three-foot bamboo sword, the *shinai*. All who practice kendo know of the resilience of the bamboo sword, its lightness, flexibility and durability. The nature of resilience embodied by the *shinai* reflects the spirit of the people in this book. That same spirit of resilience is infused in contemporary kendo, but it is usually concealed. With that in mind, I would like to take you on a journey, to explore the life and times of the pioneers of Canadian kendo, especially during World War II.

It has been almost 45 years since I immigrated to Canada, and I have been practicing kendo the entire time I have lived here, up to the present day. It has been my good fortune to meet and study kendo with many wonderful people who have become my friends. The people I present in this book are primarily kendo pioneers and my *senpai* (seniors) and fellow *kenshi* (kendo practitioners). Those who practiced kendo in the prewar period and are still living today are well over 90 years old and many have now passed away. As I have come to appreciate the value of my *senpai*'s historical account of kendo, I feel a particular urgency to collect this history in writing.

I consider it worthwhile to retrace the footsteps of our *senpai* who lived to the fullest, both wisely and resiliently, even as their lives were undermined by racial prejudice in a land that was sometimes hostile to them.

Although kendo has its roots in Japan, branches of the traditional martial art sprang up overseas long before World War II, wherever Japanese people migrated: mainly North America, the Hawaiian Islands, and Brazil. In these places, kendo has survived for over a century, sometimes barely visible beneath the surface. This is my attempt to follow one of its "branches", so to speak, through the history of kendo in Canada, where I myself immigrated.

In Chapter One, I discuss kendo in Canada during World War II, a period I personally find very interesting and significant from the perspective of kendo's development in this country.

Chapter Two jumps back in time to examine kendo activities during the prewar period, which was key to the establishment of kendo in British Columbia.

Chapter Three examines how kendo spread across Canada with the eastward movement of Japanese Canadians to Ontario and Quebec and other provinces due to government policies kept in place after the war. It also serves as a review of kendo activities from the postwar period up to the year 2000.

Chapter Four compares two distinguished kendoka, Canadian-born Motoo Matsushita and Japanese-born Torao Mori, during the development of kendo in Canada and the US before and after the war. Their contribution to North American kendo is unique and significant, particularly Torao Mori's dream and efforts, which contributed to establishing the World Kendo Champion-ships, a triennial tournament which saw the participation of 56 countries and regions in the 17th edition in 2018. As of 2020 there are 59 countries and regions affiliated with the International Kendo Federation that are eligible to participate in the World Kendo Championships.

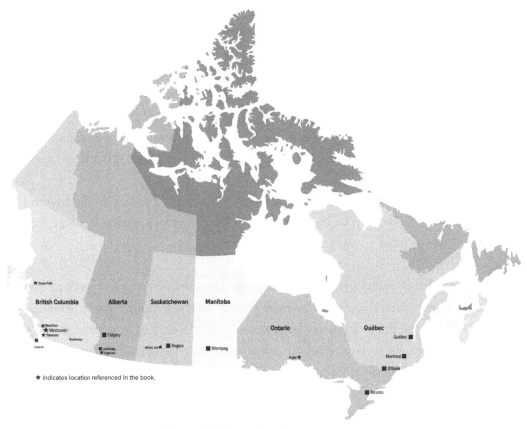

Figure 1-1: Map of Canada

CHAPTER ONE

Kendo During World War II

The first sections of this chapter cover historical information about the forced removal of Japanese Canadians—sometimes referred to as Nikkei (people of Japanese descent)—during World War II and the POW camps where some were incarcerated. I feel it is important, as it is these events that made kendo history in Canada distinctive when compared to other countries. The later sections will shed light on the various kendo clubs that emerged in the internment camps. I interviewed several people who are normally reluctant to talk about their experiences during that terrible time. I greatly appreciate the input of these individuals.

The Forced Removal of Japanese Canadians

"Lights and neon signs illuminating tall buildings that had been brilliantly lit until the night before they were extinguished, plunging the whole city into darkness. As suspicion grew that the Japanese might stage something under the cover of darkness, hatred toward the Japanese mounted, and shops operating in Caucasian districts had their windows shattered one after another…"[1]

Immigrants from Japan to Canada began arriving in British Columbia in the late 1800s drawn by the promise of work in the fishing, logging, and mining industries. From the time of their arrival, Japanese immigrants faced discrimination and hostility. Politicians and the media regularly whipped up anti-Japanese sentiment and campaigned for the removal of Japanese Canadians from British Columbia.

Following the Imperial Japanese Navy's attack on Pearl Harbor on December 7, 1941, life changed almost overnight. Japanese Canadians, regardless of their place of birth, found themselves exposed to the hostile gaze of their neighbours, some of whom who had until then been friendly.

All Japanese Canadians, regardless of their place of birth or nationality, were treated as enemy aliens. Community leaders were arrested. The government confiscated all properties, including houses, businesses, fishing boats, farms, cameras, and automobiles, later to be sold off for a

---

1   Angler P.O.W. Camp Shoko Dojo Members, *Akeyuku shoko*, p.62.

pittance without the owners' consent.

Although the Royal Canadian Mounted Police (RCMP) and Canadian military advised that Japanese Canadians posed no security threat, a 100-mile "protected area" was established along the west coast. Beginning in early 1942, over 23,000 Canadians of Japanese ancestry living in coastal British Columbia were forcibly uprooted and relocated 100 miles (160 km) away from the coast.

Most were given short notice, sometimes just a few hours, to take with them what they could carry. Over 8,000 Japanese Canadians living outside the lower mainland were processed through Hastings Park, where they were housed in animal barns while they waited to learn their destinations.

Able-bodied males between the ages of 18 and 45 were ordered to report to road camps, while women, children, and the elderly were told to prepare to be sent to internment camps in the interior of the province. Some families who had the means to support themselves elected to relocate to "self-supporting" camps in the interior of BC. Some families who wanted to stay together chose to go to sugar beet fields in Alberta and Manitoba, where they essentially served as slave labour. Men who protested the separation of families were sent to POW camps in Ontario. Although the policy of separating families was rescinded after about six months, the damage to the community was profound.

Photo 1-1: Confiscated Japanese Canadian-owned fishing vessels. Half of the 1300 boats were damaged or sunk due to rough handling, and the rest were sold off far below market value. Many of the Japanese immigrants were fishermen.

Angler POW Camp #101

It should be noted that the Japanese Canadian men imprisoned in the Angler POW camp were not combatants captured in battle. Instead, they included community leaders who were considered potential threats, and protesters who refused to report to the road camps. Also incarcerated were members of the so-called Nisei Mass Evacuation Group, a group of Nisei (second generation Japanese Canadian) youth who protested to the Canadian government that "forced internment should be carried out in family units".

Angler was a former military facility surrounded by three layers of barbed wire fences with searchlights and guards armed with heavy machine guns keeping watch atop six watch towers. A remote place, it was situated on the shores Lake Superior, the largest of North America's five Great Lakes, accessible in those days by a railroad. At its peak, it held over 700 Japanese Canadian prisoners.

Photo 1-2: Group photo in front of part of the Angler facilities.

Photo 1-3: At the Angler POW camp. After morning roll call, inmates bow to the East or to the sun to pay their respects. I was not able to confirm the frequency and its purpose.

The time spent in the Angler varied from person to person, with the majority incarcerated for four and a half years—from the start of the war until eight months after it ended.

Life in a POW Camp

"We have become passengers of a military train heading who knows where guarded by fully-armed Canadian soldiers. But just what kind of crime have we committed against Canada? Is it such a big crime to express disagreement with the misplaced relocation policy of an administration and demand to be relocated at least in family units?"[2]

Much of the information on this period is provided by Robert Katsumasa Okazaki in his 1996 book *The Nisei Mass Evacuation Group and P.O.W. '101', Angler, Ontario*, which is the English version of his Japanese-language book, *Angura, Ontario Senji horyo shuyojo*, published in 1992. The two books, which share similar but not identical content, give us a glimpse into the mindset of a Canadian Nisei.

Photo 1-4: Mess hall of the Angler POW camp. Notice that on the back of the prisoner's uniform, there is a large red circle, which was intended to be used by prison guards as a visual target should the prisoner attempt to escape.

2   Okazaki, Robert K., *Angura, Ontario Senji horyo shuyojo #101*, p.60.

Okazaki, who was one of the kendo practitioners at Angler, wrote the original book after the war based on a precious journal and other materials he kept while he worked in the camp office. He took careful notes of what went on at the camp, adding his own observations. The work is full of data about the activities and lives of the men at the camp, all arranged in a journal format. Compared to the Germans who had been captured in combat and were interned in adjacent facilities, the Japanese Canadians, as non-combatants, enjoyed relatively more freedom of movement as well as free time, even though they remained within the securely guarded grounds of the camp.

Within the camp, the Nikkei men organized themselves into 14 sections, managing facilities such as a secretariat, concessions store, dining room, library, barbershop, and fire brigade, as well as services such as ration distribution, mail, academics, physical education, sewing, mending, and shoe repair. Entertainment and physical education included everything from kendo, judo, and baseball. There were also brass band, *go*, and *haiku* clubs, and a wide variety of groups providing things such as Japanese lessons for the Nisei and English lessons for the Issei. Among the 700 men there, many were talented and capable of teaching others. At least one (possibly more) University of British Columbia students were also imprisoned at Angler after being expelled from the school. What is interesting is that marching Japanese military-style, led by veterans of the Russo-Japanese War, was recognized as one of the physical education activities.

The men lived in dormitories, 80 to each building, furnished with rows of bunk beds. Their daily life began with wake-up at 6:30, breakfast at 6:45, clean-up activities from 9:00 to 11:30, lunch at 12:00, work details from 13:30 to 16:30, supper at 17:00 and ended with lights out at 22:30.

Some of the men had been influenced by Japanese militarism. These included not only Issei who had come from Japan and the *kika-nisei* who had returned to Canada after receiving education in Japan, but also Nisei who had never been to Japan. Many apparently still had faith in the victory of the "divine nation" of Japan. These men were called *ganbari-ya* (roughly "hard liners"). However, most of the Canadian-educated Nisei seem to have had cooler heads. Clearly, this was a collection of men with many different ideas about the war. Some gathered information on the war's progress from newspapers that those assigned to cleaning-up the quarters of the non-commissioned officer guards would bring back tucked under their clothing, according to Okazaki's book.

One thing all the men shared was constant hunger, as the meals they provided were never enough. From Okazaki's journal:

1944, January 1. As busy as my day-to-day life in this internment camp is, the passage of time has been very fast, today being my second *shogatsu* [New Year's Day] here already . . . Our big enemy are the daily snowstorms and the cold that is constantly with us. But the rousing cries of our young men engaged in judo and kendo workouts ringing out on this shore of Lake Superior are stirring . . . Our daily meals consisted mainly of a potato and two slices of bread but occasionally we were also given an egg or mutton stew. But what we enjoyed most was the taste of rice that was served once in a while. There was a lot of barley mixed in as well, but the familiar taste of rice was so good that it almost had me in tears.[3]

Japanese foods including soy sauce and miso were sent to the camps from time to time by the Japanese Red Cross.

---

3   Okazaki, Robert K., *Angura, Ontario Senji horyo shuyojo #101*, p.162.

Kendo in a POW Camp

Shoko Kenshi

The Shoko Dojo was a kendo club set up in a recreation hall at Angler. The "*Sho*" of Shoko comes from the name of the head instructor, Motoo [pronounced Mo-to-o] Matsushita. "*Sho*" is an alternate reading of "*matsu*" meaning "pine tree", and "*ko*" meaning "lake", which comes from the fact that it was located on the shore of Lake Superior. So, Shoko was named after both the sensei and location of their club. The dedicated men that founded this club and kept it going for two-and-a-half years called themselves the "Shoko Kenshi" (Shoko Swordsmen). Most of these men—separated from their families, with their properties confiscated, and held in isolation—were able to turn these negative circumstances into something admirably positive. With a stretch of imagination, the two years and several months of the kendo club's activities could be considered a training camp of an unprecedented duration. At the same time, it was a period when each man had to quietly endure a myriad of sentiments, such as longing for their families.

Photo 1-5: Group photo of Shoko Dojo kendo club. Believed to have been taken on August 22, 1944, on the first anniversary of the club's founding. The building in the background of photo is the recreation hall where kendo practices took place. As the possession of cameras was strictly forbidden at the camp, the photos must have been taken by the Canadian military. Only some of the men are wearing proper kendo *bogu* and *hakama*.

Matsushita-sensei

The main founder of the Shoko Dojo was Motoo Matsushita, a Nisei. Matsushita was sent to Japan to be educated. He attended Maebashi Commercial High School in Gunma Prefecture and practiced with the school kendo club. Upon graduation in 1936, at the age of 19, he returned to his native Canada. Although he was fairly young, as someone who had received proper kendo training in Japan, he began serving as head instructor of kendo at Woodfibre and Vancouver around 1936. In 1942, when he was 25, Matsushita was sent to the Angler POW camp, where he

Photo 1-6: Kendo match at Angler POW Camp. Believed to have been taken on August 22, 1944, on the first anniversary of the club's founding.

Photo 1-7: Kenshi watching and waiting for their bouts.

was imprisoned until his release at age 29. Shortly after his arrival at Angler, Matsushita began his efforts to set up a kendo club in the camp.

Negotiation

The book *The Dawning of Pine Lake* (Akeyuku Shoko), details kendo at Angler. Handmade from materials available in the camp, the book consists of short, handwritten essays written by Shoko Kenshi, and a detailed account of a kendo championship that was held one year after the kendo club was established. Over 360 pages in length, this rare book is an invaluable resource which allows us to access the "real voices" of these Shoko Kenshi, and get a clear picture the hardships and conditions involved in setting up the club. The editor, it can be assumed, was primarily assistant instructor Katashi Hibi, with other members helping.

So, we negotiated right away through our spokesman for permission, which was given, to hold kendo training and for the delivery of equipment.

At the time, Matsushita-sensei was overjoyed. Thus, the kendo club was born under Head Instructor Matsushita on August 22 [1943].

The preparations and the negotiations with the military authorities until then took a lot of effort to say the least.

Here in the East [Province of Ontario], the military personnel had never been in contact with Japanese people at all. As it was for the very first time, it was extremely difficult to make them understand our demands and explanations.

The circumstances were such that even the Nisei folk had never seen kendo and did not know anything about its equipment, so it would seem only natural that Caucasians in the East of Canada found it hard to comprehend what kendo was all about even as we tried. After we kept insisting and explaining that kendo was a kind of sport similar to the fencing in their own country, we finally obtained permission.[4]

---

4   Angler P.O.W. Camp Shoko Dojo Members, *Akeyuku shoko*, p.66.

Birch Shinai—Kendo Equipment at Angler

Practicing kendo requires specialized equipment, which was of course not available in the wilds of Ontario. Shoko Kenshi were fortunate to have *shinai* sent to them after Matsushita-sensei and others contacted friends for help. The YMCA, among others, came to their aid. They initially received two sets of *bogu* (protective armour) and 10 *shinai* that had been in use before the war. In the end, they were able to get 12 sets of armour and 29 *shinai*. Over time the *shinai* broke so they were forced to make their own, which was difficult without access to bamboo.

Okazaki's book details how the Shoko Kenshi made their own *shinai* from birch and repaired *bogu*, and how they practiced kendo using this equipment.

> Having spent a considerable number of days training under the guidance of Renshi 4-dan Motoo Matsushita-sensei, starting with the true essence of basic kendo and *kendo kata*, there was not a single usable bamboo *shinai* left.

> The wooden *shinai* (normally made from bamboo) the keen kenshi produced by splitting the birch branches are very finely crafted. But these *shinai* have a drawback. As they are several times heavier, when one is struck by one, the impact can be felt.

> The birchwood *shinai* are made by shaving suitable parts of the wood to an appropriate thickness, curing them in the shade, whittling them down to the correct size and, for the finish, smoothing out the surface roughness with glass powder.

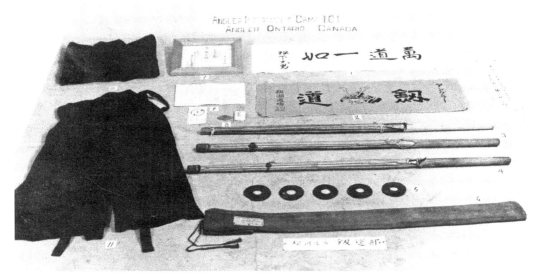

Photo 1-8: Items made by hand at the camp. Training wear—*hakama* made from sugar sacks, *shinai* from birch branches, and *tsuba* from shoe leather.

Their action is further improved by rubbing oil or wax into them. It is quite a cumbersome process but because all kendo club members take part, they are virtually an "unlimited company".[5]

In addition to the *shinai*, the kenshi had to share the armour, which they repaired frequently. They also had to make *hakama* and *shinai* sheaths from flour sacks, *tsuba* from shoe leather, *kendo-gi* from sugar sacks, and so on. Moreover, they did not even have proper tools for crafting these items, which makes their dedication all the more remarkable.

Training

Sections of *Senji Horyo Shuuyoujo* describe the evaluation of individual pupils' kendo that encourages them by discussing the state of mind at the high level of contemporary 4-dan and 5-dan kenshi.

> The way our kenshi train entails a degree of seriousness that is probably not seen anywhere else. Kendo at Angler that was started in order to teach kendo positions and to train both the mind and the body, has gathered together many men, including those in their teens as well as their 40s and 50s, so that for four days every week, they fill the entertainment hall with unbounded enthusiasm that makes the hall feel too small. They are required to learn 17 kinds of *men-waza*, 13 kinds of *kote-waza*, eight kinds of *do-waza* and 10 kinds of *tsuki-waza*, as well as refereeing techniques necessary for this martial art, so it is all quite time consuming.[6]

Observing Kendo by Government Officials

Around 1943, senior officers representing the Canadian government requested to observe a kendo training session. Below is an excerpt from *Akeyuku shoko*.

> When a Major Roberts, the Secretary of State and other senior officials were visiting us, they asked to observe our kendo training. For the visiting senior officials, kendo was a world unheard of and unseen…

> …when Matsushita-sensei fought against Hibi, and other *dan*-level men, they demonstrated a highly-charged version of *kakari-geiko* [short, intense, attack practice], the officials were astounded and terribly impressed. They were so favourably impressed that

---

5   Okazaki, Robert K., *Angura, Ontario Senji horyo shuyojo #101*, p.180.
6   Okazaki, Robert K., *Angura, Ontario Senji horyo shuyojo #101*, p.180–181.

they delivered words of praise for this great sport for boosting the morale of the citizens and building up their strength….

… they were also reported to have said they would like to encourage it for Canadians. In the not-too-distant future, an era will surely arrive when kendo will take a major leap forward as a worldwide sport.

The significance of the fact that they were able to give the visitors an extremely favourable impression, that is to say succeeding in presenting the unique, traditional Japanese martial art of kendo to senior Canadian officials, then a country at war with Japan, seemed profound to say the least. At the same time, we have truly recognised that for us to return to the frontline of the challenge to propagate our kendo in the new, better century the world is the duty of us Nikkei Nisei who were born in a foreign country. We have no choice but to accept the seriousness of this duty.[7]

Those words proved to be visionary, as roughly 70 years later, in 2015, the 16th World Kendo Championships took place in Tokyo with the participation of 56 countries and regions. Looking back at these writings, collected over 70 years ago by a Japanese Canadian Nisei confined in a POW internment camp, it is quite moving in view of the time and place in which they were put to paper.

Ten days following Japan's defeat, a championship commemorating the second anniversary of the founding of Shoko Dojo took place in the camp. The following are quotes from Okazaki's book.

August 14, 1945
Japan has survived many bombings, but the two atomic bombs have convinced the Emperor that his people should not suffer any longer. We had to presume Japan has surrendered and ended the war.

August 26, 1946
Summer is almost gone. The kenshi have been training diligently, and we held our second, and likely last, tournament in the Shoko Dojo. The bouts were not strictly win or lose, but clean-cut *waza* surfaced throughout the matches! Our spectators were surprised and awe-struck as the *shiai* showed the use of *nito-ryu* and *naginata*. The perpetual mending and patching of our worn-out kendo-gu [*bogu*] and many hours of practice have paid off for us.[8]

---

7   Angler P.O.W. Camp Shoko Dojo Members, *Akeyuku shoko*, p.47.
8   Okazaki, Robert K., *The Nisei Mass Evacuation Group and P.O.W. '101', Angler, Ontario*, p.116.

A training period of two and half years is not long, but it would be safe to assume that the content of the training was quite substantial, as they participated in a *gasshuku*-like regimen under the leadership of Motoo Matsushita. In kendo and other sports, *gasshuku* means a camp which provide intense training session, where members of a dojo would focus on their skills. At Angler, with little else to do during their forced confinement, the *gasshuku* lasted two-and-a-half years, which is quite a remarkable length for a training session.

At this point, I would like to list some relevant events related to Shoko Dojo activities in chronological order.

December 7, 1941	Attack on Pearl Harbor
July 21, 1942	Internment at Angler
June 16, 1943	Formal establishment of Shoko Dojo kendo club
July 9, 1944	Training competition
August 20, 1944	Championship commemorating 1st anniversary of club's establishment
August 14, 1945	Japan's surrender (Canada time)
August 26, 1945	Championship commemorating 2nd anniversary of the club's establishment
April 29, 1946	Closure of internment camp, release of last group of internees

Kendo Clubs at Internment Camps in British Columbia

Around the same time that kendo was being practiced at the Angler POW camp in Ontario, kendo clubs were formed in a number of internment camps in the interior of British Columbia.

Internment camps

As the result of the Canadian government's wartime policy of removing Japanese Canadians from the west coast, the majority were sent to abandoned mining towns or to privately-owned farmland, where crude shacks were built. There were more than 10 locations, all located 100 miles (160 km) or more from the British Columbia coast. The majority were situated in the Kootenay region of the province. Although security was light, compared to the POW camps, conditions were primitive. The internees, dressed in their finest city clothes, were unprepared for the harsh conditions. Due to the accelerated timeline of the internment, housing was not ready when the first internees arrived, and they were forced to live in tents amid winter temperatures as low as 20 degrees below zero, Celsius.

Photo 1-9: Rows of temporary tent accommodations, Bay Farm, Slocan, BC at the beginning of the internment.

Later, under the government's direction, internees made timber from local trees and used it to construct shacks. Because the green wood did not have time to cure, it shrank in the winter, leaving large gaps. Without insulation, ice would form on the insides of the shacks. Kitchens, toilets, and hot baths were mostly shared. It was not easy living with two or more families to a hut with only fabric for partitions. It is reported that in the beginning, there were constant

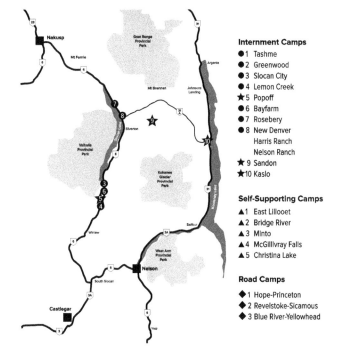

Internment Camps

- ●1 Tashme
- ●2 Greenwood
- ●3 Slocan City
- ●4 Lemon Creek
- ★5 Popoff
- ●6 Bayfarm
- ●7 Rosebery
- ●8 New Denver
  Harris Ranch
  Nelson Ranch
- ★9 Sandon
- ★10 Kaslo

Self-Supporting Camps

- ▲1 East Lillooet
- ▲2 Bridge River
- ▲3 Minto
- ▲4 McGillivray Falls
- ▲5 Christina Lake

Road Camps

- ◆1 Hope-Princeton
- ◆2 Revelstoke-Sicamous
- ◆3 Blue River-Yellowhead

Detail map of Kootenay area with internment camps indicated
★ indicates location referenced in the book.

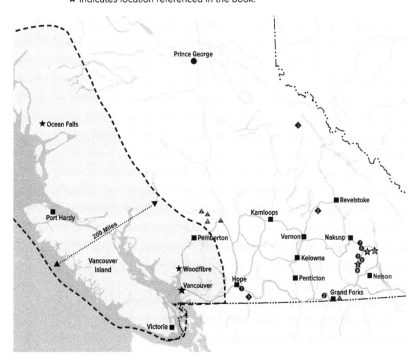

Map of British Columbia with internment camps, self-supporting camps
and road camps indicated. ★ indicates location referenced in the book.

Figure 1-2: BC Internment Camps located a minimum 100 miles (160 kilometers) beyond the British Columbia coastline.

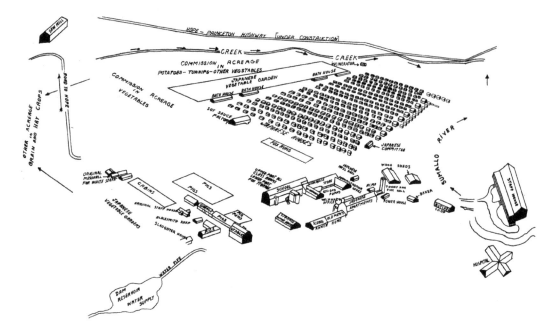

Figure 1-3: Groups of Residential Huts at Tashme relocation site. Two families were interned in each hut.

quarrels between housewives. In comparison, the internment camps in the US for American Nikkei were fenced in and internees were provided with housing and meals, but in Canada the internees had to take care of their own food and clothing. There were some jobs that provided low wages and some welfare assistance was available.

To their credit, the internees did not just sit around bemoaning their hardship. As they gradually settled down in their new lives, they formed self-governing bodies to run the camps. Vegetable gardens were planted, *ofuro* (community baths) were built, and schools were set up.

Various recreational activities, including kendo, were set up to pass the time. Kendo was taught to youth and children by several sensei from Steveston, a fishing village at the mouth of the Fraser River in British Columbia and the home of kendo in Canada. Kendo was taught at three BC internment camps—Kaslo, Popoff and Sandon. A sensei from Steveston also taught kendo in Raymond, Alberta. Steveston will be discussed further in Chapter Two.

Kaslo

Kaslo, a ghost town, is located on the shores of Kootenay Lake. Internees arrived on the steam ship SS Nasookin. During internment there were approximately 1,100 internees, which made up two-thirds of the town's population. The BC Security Commission leased 52 buildings, which they reconditioned, along with 30 acres for gardens. They provided work in wood cutting, construction, maintenance, and gardening. Kaslo School was the first of the camp schools to open in September 1942. *The New Canadian,* the only Japanese-Canadian newspaper allowed to be printed during the war years, was published in Kaslo.

SS.Nasookin unloading Jap Evacuees at Kaslo B.C. Mar 11 1942

Photo1-10: Scene of disembarkation upon arrival in Kaslo. Japanese Canadians were transported to Kaslo by train and then by boat.

A dojo called Yoseikan (養正館) was established taking its name from a dojo set up in Steveston before the war by Rintaro Hayashi, Shichiro Takahashi and Seiichiro Mizuguchi. Over 60 boys and 20 girls in Kaslo were taught the basics and *kata* for about three years.

The Yoseikan *dojo-kun* (rules) could well be Hayashi's interpretation of bushido, as expressed in his teachings. Hayashi strove to engender a higher sense of morality in boys and girls, even during life in an internment camp.

Guiding Principles of Kendo Training (Yoseikan Dojo Rules)

- Respect manners, and do not be complacent or cowardly in your actions.
- Honour and reputation matter most in a samurai's life. One aspiring toward these must not be double-faced and must refrain from treacherous acts.
- Value deference and kindness and never give in to the strong or look down on the weak or make light of those who do not know the way of the sword or compete with them for fame and honour.
- Strive for gentleness, refrain from competitiveness as much as possible, and do not get involved in quarrels or personal fights.
- Modesty is a source of strength; vanity is a source of weakness. Refrain from frivolous and lewd acts.
- Weapons are lethal. Using them for a just cause is a virtue in martial arts but using them for an unjust cause is violence in martial arts.
- Instructors must be treated with all due respect. Obey what they teach, follow their orders, and cultivate the practice of discipline and temperance.[9]

Photo1-11: Yoseikan Kendo Club male members at Kaslo (Rintaro Hayashi Collection). The person in the middle of the second row is Rintaro Hayashi, then age 43. This photo was taken in 1944.

---

9   Hayashi Rintaro private collection

Photo1-12: Yoseikan Kendo Club female members at Kaslo.

Popoff

Popoff was built on leased farmland and was one of the internment camps that made up what was known as the Slocan extension. The other camps in the Slocan extension included Bay Farm, Slocan City, and Lemon Creek. By December 1942, 932 Japanese Canadians were listed as living there. The camp was located at the southern end of Slocan Lake which narrowed into the Slocan River. Kendo dojo Slocan Yoshinkan (養神館) was founded and taught by Kanzaburo Kobayashi. Later on, Masao Hayashi relocated to Popoff and joined the dojo.

Sandon

Sandon was once Canada's richest silver mining community but was a ghost town by the time it was repurposed to house Japanese Canadian internees. Accessible only by a narrow mountain road and a railway for transporting the silver, the place was narrow and in shadow, surrounded by towering mountains.

A 23-acre farm a mile away from town was the only means of self-support for the internees. The Japanese Canadian population was 933 by November 1942. In December 1942, the Sandon School was the second internment camp school to open. Employment was scarce but many internees were elderly, including Japanese Canadian WWI veterans. The population of Sandon was mostly Buddhist. Kendo was taught by Masao Hayashi, a younger brother of Rintaro Hayashi, before he relocated to Popoff.

Photo 1-13: Judging from the background, they constructed the building behind them by themselves using lumber from trees they had felled. There is a note in the photo marking the occasion of Spring tournament on April 1, 1945. This photo is believed to have been taken at Popoff.

Photo 1-14: The grown-ups probably told the boys to pose, but their postures are quite good, nevertheless. The huge tree stumps in the background tell their own story. This photo is believed to have been taken at Popoff.

Photo 1-15: Children facing off during a kendo session at Sandon, BC.

Photo 1-16: boys preparing for kendo in Sandon.

Raymond, Alberta

During the war, some Japanese Canadians were sent to sugar beet farms in Alberta, Manitoba, and Ontario to work as cheap labour, with the promise that families could stay together. As of November 1942, the Nikkei population of the sugar beet projects totaled 3,991, with Alberta taking the largest number of beet farming families. A total of 2,588 people lived in communities including Vauxhall, Iron Springs, Taber, Picture Butte, Coaldale, Raymond, and Magrath, all of which were near Lethbridge, Alberta. Families were housed in poorly insulated shacks that did little to keep out the extreme cold. Many did not last long in this harsh climate.

Kendo was taught in Raymond at the Buddhist Church by Yuichi Akune (1909-1995), the former sensei of Steveston Kendo Club. Roy Akune, a son of Yuichi Akune, describes its activity:

> In retrospect, the move to Raymond from Iron Springs, Alberta in November 1943 was most significant to the Akune family. The move to Raymond was prompted by an invitation from the leaders of the Raymond Buddhist Temple and the temple minister, Rev. Shinjo Ikuta, to organize the kendo club. Rev. Ikuta, who was minister of the New Westminster Buddhist Temple prior to the WWII internment of the Japanese and who had known about Yuichi's leadership in Kendo in Steveston and other nearby dojo, became a strong proponent of him to lead the Club.

> The kendo club, along with the judo club that was organised at the same, were designed to be a major part of the Temple youth programme. Both kendo and judo became very popular. In the fall, after the harvesting of sugar beets was completed—usually in October—kendo practices would resume and were held weekly on the second floor made of hardwood while judo was practiced on the main floor. I, too, would join with the aspirants and undergo rigorous practices on Friday nights and, at times, during the week. These Friday nights were fun nights for us as they became friendship gatherings. Annual tournaments were also held. Arrangements were made with the Federal Security Commission authorities for the equipment to be shipped from Steveston. The *bogu*, kendo equipment, was stored in the attic of our home on Trites Road in Steveston. Enough equipment was assembled that many of the kenshi were fully armoured.[10]

---

10 Ron Akune to author: February 20, 2020.

Redress

In this chapter, I have discussed Japanese Canadian interment during war time. It is notable that in the late 1970s, more than 30 years after the end of the war, Japanese Canadians, mostly Nisei and Sansei, launched a nationwide campaign called "The Redress Movement". They demanded that the Canadian government offer an apology for the unjust wartime actions against Japanese and Canadians of Japanese descent, alongside individual financial compensation for the wartime damage and losses. On September 22, 1988, then-Prime Minister Brian Mulroney officially announced an apology, along with individual and community compensation for the wartime policies levied against the Nikkei. The financial compensation was largely symbolic, given the actual losses, but together with the apology, it set the stage for the rejuvenation of the community and the recovery of honour and respect that was lost during the wartime years.

However, I would like to end the wartime stories with a question. How did these pioneers possess so much passion for kendo, considering the great hardships they endured during the war? I believe it was because of over 30 years of kendo activity before the war, a period when Japanese immigration was still in its pioneering stage.

CHAPTER TWO

Prewar Development

The Dawn of Kendo in Canada

The dawn of kendo in Canada goes back to the turn of the 20th century. It is likely that as Japanese immigrants began to enjoy a measure of comfort in their lives, men began to practice kendo in small groups, here and there. If that was its dawn, the pinnacle would have to be around the time of the formation of the Association of Canadian Kendo Dan-Holders, about six months before the start of Japan's involvement in World War II in 1941. The formation of the association took place just a little over 30 years after kendo was introduced to Canada, showing how those pioneers were devoted to kendo. Although this golden age of kendo in Canada lasted only a short time, it was an important period that led to the practice of kendo during wartime.

Prewar Immigration and Historical Background

Most of the early Japanese immigrants came from farming or fishing villages in Japan. Known as *dekasegi* (those going overseas to make money), most intended to return to their villages after having made their fortune. Although the early new arrivals were almost exclusively young men, they soon sent for wives and started to raise families in Canada.

The early immigrants gravitated to wherever there was work, and small communities soon formed throughout British Columbia. There were two main centres of activity, both in the southern part of the province. The village of Steveston, situated at the mouth of the Fraser River, was the centre of the fishing industry and soon had a thriving Japanese Canadian community, complete with its own hospital. A large Japanese neighborhood also formed in the Powell Street area in Vancouver's East Side. Powell Street was a bustling section of town with many bathhouses, hotels, Japanese-style inns, and other businesses. Schools, churches, and other organizations served as gathering places.

From the beginning, Japanese Canadians ran into cultural and linguistic barriers, and racial discrimination was a fact of daily life. In 1907, discrimination against Asians was reaching its peak. In what became known as the 1907 Riot, a large mob of Caucasians gathered and attacked Chinatown and the Powell Street neighbourhood. After marching through Chinatown, smashing shop windows and ransacking the interiors, they met resistance in the Japanese quarters, and were driven away with stones, bricks and sticks. Fortunately, there were no deaths or serious injuries, but the incident eventually led to restrictions being placed on Japanese migration with Japan and Canada signing the Lemieux Agreement in 1907.

Because Japanese Canadians were denied the right to vote, they were barred from most professions including the civil service and teaching. While some started businesses catering to Japanese Canadians in enclaves such as Powell Street and Steveston, the majority turned to resource industries for their livelihoods.

Many Japanese immigrants were initially drawn to the west coast of Canada by the abundance of fish, particularly salmon. Smaller Nikkei communities formed up and down the coast, generally located around the canneries that controlled much of the industry. Many of the men fished for the canneries, while the women worked on the canning lines.

Resentment towards Japanese Canadians for their initial success in the fishing industry eventually led to a drastic reduction of fishing licenses allotted to them. So, many turned to farming instead. A heavy demand for strawberries during World War I encouraged many of the farmers to grow this lucrative crop. Families would buy forested land and clear it using dynamite, horses, and hand tools. Before World War II, there were over 500 Japanese Canadian farmers living and working along the Fraser River in the Fraser Valley, some of British Columbia's most fertile agricultural land. The success of the farmers led to the formation of several Japanese Canadian

Photo 2-1: Parade participants celebrating the Royal Visit on the 300 block of Powell Street, Vancouver, BC, 1939.

Photo 2-2: Kidokan Judo/Kendo Dojo in Haney, BC, built in 1936. Many immigrants encouraged their children to practice martial arts in order to engender traditional Japanese discipline and spirit. This dojo was built by Japanese farmers in the farming village of Haney, 50km from Vancouver.

Photo 2-3: Fisherman's village, Steveston circa 1928. As indicated in the photo, laundry was hung in front of these houses, where people lived with their families.

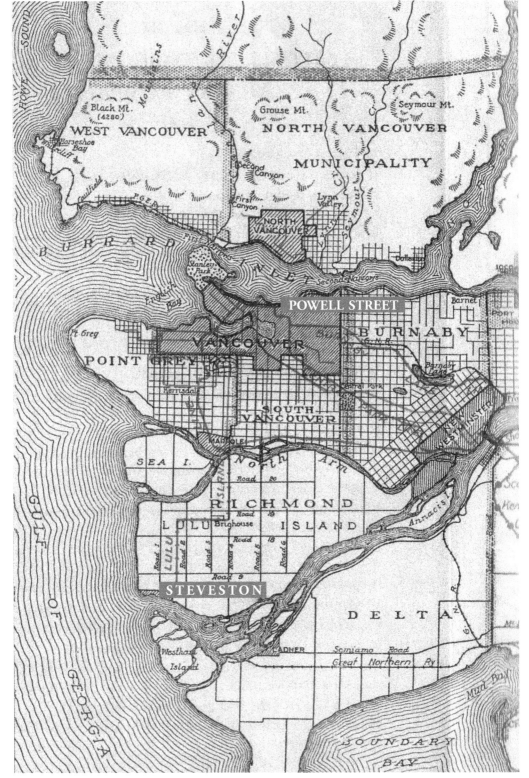

Figure 2-1: Map of Vancouver and Steveston in 1930 with Steveston and Powell Street highlighted.

farmer associations. Other Japanese Canadians found work and formed communities in the logging and mining industries throughout British Columbia and in southern Alberta.

In their spare time, Japanese Canadians engaged in leisure activities including baseball, hockey, music, and dance. The various martial arts practiced included judo, sumo and kendo. Prior to the war, kendo was practiced exclusively by Japanese Canadians. Many of them first had to earn their living as fishermen, lumberjacks, farmers, and sawmill and pulp mill workers. They practiced kendo in their spare time. As many of the early practitioners were fishermen, it was natural that Yokikan, the very first kendo dojo, was established in Steveston where numerous Nikkei fishermen and their families lived. During the fishing season, kendo was suspended—it was livelihood first.

Rintaro Hayashi (1902-1995) and His Writings

Born in the village of Mio in Wakayama prefecture, Rintaro Hayashi arrived in Canada as a boy in 1913 and became a fisherman when a young man. Over his lifetime he was very active in the Nikkei fishing community. By the 1920s, Japanese Canadian fishermen held over half of the government-issued fishing licenses. Through pressure from Caucasian and indigenous fishermen, over 1,000 Japanese Canadians had their licenses revoked. Hayashi was among those who fought these discriminatory practices in the Supreme Court of Canada and the Privy Council of England, although they were ultimately unsuccessful.

Following the attack on Pearl Harbor, Hayashi was interned in Kaslo for the duration of the war. As discussed in the previous chapter, he organized a kendo club in the camp. Returning to Steveston in 1950, Hayashi resumed fishing. He was among the members of the Nikkei community who built the Steveston Community Centre, which was completed in 1957. He also helped re-establish the Steveston Kendo Club with Yuichi Akune and worked to build a *budokan* (martial arts centre) there in 1972. He became a director of the first Canadian Kendo Federation.

In 1967, he wrote *An Outline of Kendo in Canada*, an unpublished manuscript that provides important information on the early days of kendo in Canada. Around the time of his retirement, Hayashi wrote two more books. Published in 1974, *Kuroshio no hate ni* (Beyond the Japanese Current) details the early history of Nikkei fishing communities. *Kouhan mandan* (Banter on the Riverside) was published in 1988, but it was not made available for general sale or distribution. It was remarkable that Hayashi was able to write *Kouhan mandan* when he was 87 years old after suffering a stroke. His right hand was incapacitated, so he painstakingly typed the book using one of the first word processors on the market. *Kouhan* (riverside) referred to the banks of the Fraser River where Steveston, his home, was located. In those days, various species of salmon would migrate upstream during the spring, summer, and fall seasons. It was these salmon that had attracted Japanese folk to this location. For the fishermen based there, the river represented everything in their lives. *Mandan* (banter), an amusing account of life and times in the day, is proof of his erudite sense of humour.

Today, the accounts of this capable writer remain the only clue as to what kendo in Canada must have been like some 100 years ago. His writing provided much of the background for this book.

Photo 2-4: Rintaro Hayashi.

The Beginning of Kendo in Canada

The following is an excerpt from *Kanada no kendo ryakushi* (An Outline of Kendo in Canada) that Hayashi distributed to his kendo friends. I obtained this from Shigeru Kuwabara, one of the Shoko Kenshi at Angler.

> The history of kendo in Canada is not very old. When the Imperial Navy's Vice-Admiral Ichiji, famous for bravery as the commander of the flagship Mikasa during the 1905 Battle of Tsushima Strait, sailed into Vancouver commanding a training fleet consisting of the ships Aso and Soya, a kendo competition was held against men and officers of the crew. It was reported that the Canadian side did not stand a chance, but it is not known who those Canadians were.
>
> In 1914 a kendo dojo named Yokikan (養気館) opened in Steveston. This was probably the very first kendo dojo in Canada. A small fishing village, Steveston is not only the Canadian Nikkei folks' place of origin but is also the place of origin of Canadian kendo.[1]

Figures at the Dawn of Kendo in Canada

Hayashi's book describes the men behind the scenes of Canadian kendo in its formative years. In those days, kendo was still called "*gekken*" (fighting swords) in Japan. It seems that Kenta

---

1   Hayashi Rintaro, *Kanada no kendo ryakushi*, p.1.

Tsuzuki and Atsumu Kamino were the founders of kendo in Canada. The following are excerpts are quoted from *Kouhan mandan*:

Kenta Tsuzuki 都築健太

How high was Mr Tsuzuki's level of kendo? At the Yushinkan Dojo (有信館) of Negishi Shingoro's Shinto Munen-ryu School in Tokyo, I heard that Mr. Tsuzuki used to be 4-kyu in a system of 10 *kyu*, 10th being the lowest *kyu* for beginners. He would therefore be about 3-dan in today's *dan* ranking. He seems to be a Yushinkan man. The reason he continues to be so highly regarded, even today in Steveston, is that there never has been a kenshi better than him here. It cannot be denied that the seeds he sowed became the Steveston Young Men's Kendo Club and became the foundation of Canada Yoseikan.

Photo 2-5: Kenta Tsuzuki.

Atsumu Kamino 神野 専

Atsumu Kamino's family has practiced kendo for generations and are in possession of the original scroll of the Ono-ha Itto-ryu school of swordsmanship.

Around 1913 or 1914, when Mr. Kenta Tsuzuki was the head instructor at the Steveston Yokikan, a young swordsman who was a *sensei* from Vancouver, a man small in stature but full of fighting spirit, would show up from time to time to train the youngsters. That was Atsumu Kamino who would later be known by his nickname of "Kaminari Oyaji" (old man of thunder). When I was around 12 or 13 years old, I used to go and watch his training sessions every night. Calling himself a *mudansha* (a kenshi with no *dan* grade), he would preside over a coterie of *dan* holders. During competitions and other bouts, he would always volunteer to referee and no one thought he was out of place.

Photo 2-6: Atsumu Kamino (right) and Teizo Koyama.

It has already been three years since Atsumu Oyaji, or "our old man Atsumu", passed away. It is very sad that we can no longer see his figure with his piercing, falcon-like gaze. But what this writer feels even more sad about is that our *oyaji* ended his life without ever winning recognition from the Canadian kendo world that he nurtured with so much enthusiasm.

When Mr. Tsuzuki, Yokikan's head instructor, subsequently left Steveston, the dojo was left without a leader and was almost to the point of disappearing. Around 1922–23, however, two men came to Canada – Hiroaki Watanabe and Teizo Koyama.

Teizo Koyama 小山貞蔵

This man established the Vancouver Yoshinkan dojo together with Mr. Atsumu Kamino. Breaking with the conventional style, he taught beginners his basic movements. It was a three-stage move, i.e. moving from *chudan* (middle stance) to *jodan* (upper stance), striking, and then returning to *chudan*. This man's contribution is huge in that he radically changed the conventional training method used in Canada. As a *shinai* technique, his special technique was *maki-otoshi* in which he would wrap his *shinai* around his opponents to pull it down, as if snatching it away.

Photo 2-7: Vancouver Yoshinkan studio photo in 1936 with sensei A. Kamino and T. Koyama Back row left, kendo pioneer Tamaichi Douglas Funamoto. Years after the war, in 1976, he started the Shidokan Kendo Club in Montreal.

At the time, kenshi in Steveston were also being trained by them. Koyama, who had trained under Hakudo Nakayama-sensei at Yushinkan, was 5-dan at the time, later becoming 6-dan.

The Yoshinkan was staffed by mid-level kenshi like Shoji, Egaki, Ichikawa, Funamoto, and Tatemichi. It was a time when Canadian kendo was gradually beginning to flourish, from the early 1930s to right before the war.[2]

George Takahara's Story in a Remote Place

What was kendo in remote areas of pre-war Canada really like? To find out, I interviewed Mr. George Takahara, a Nisei born in 1921. He began practicing kendo at Ocean Falls, BC, from first to sixth grade before being sent to Japan to stay with his grandparents in order to receive a Japanese education. Ocean Falls, the largest pulp and paper mill in British Columbia, was built in 1921 along with a town for its workers. It is located some 430 km north of Vancouver, to which it used to take two days and two nights to travel to by ferry, he recalled.

There were about 30 families, as well as single men, totalling around 300 Japanese. In those days, Nikkei would form communities wherever there was work.

According to Mr. Takahara's recollection, discipline during kendo practice was very severe. To be flipped over or pushed over was considered routine, and the atmosphere was such that it was no use complaining to one's instructor or parents. The worst was practicing in the cold, he said. The dojo was nothing like the well-built facilities of today, but just an ordinary meeting hall with wooden floorboards. The temperature there would drop to under -30°C in winter. There was of course no heating, so the boys would tuck their bare feet under the hems of the long *hakama* to stand on the ice-cold floor, hoping their instructor would not notice. When they put on their *men*, they would hear the crackling of ice, which was frozen perspiration from the previous day's training.

It must have been physically demanding on the boys to train in an old meeting hall using adult-size protective equipment. The kendo instructor was a pastor at the Nikkei church named Reverend Kabayama. If they missed kendo practices, they still had to go to church on Sundays with their parents, so there was no place to escape in that environment. Recalling those days gone by, Mr. Takahara said that kendo was one thing he never lost at, even when he was going to school in Japan, thanks to this rigorous training.

---

2   Hayashi Rintaro, *Kouhan mandan*, p.126-130.

Kendo's Prewar Golden Age

Prewar Kendo Competitions in Photos

Various kendo tournaments were held from the late 1920s to 1941, including championships involving US clubs, which seem to have been held on an annual basis during this period as shown in the following photos.

Photo 2-8 was taken in 1931. This was before the golden age period so the number of participants was smaller than a decade later during the pinnacle of the golden age. This was around the time when the kendo population had grown enough to hold a competition. It appears to be the first joint kendo meet of Yoseikan, Steveston and Yoshinkan, Vancouver. Thereafter, it seems various kinds of competitive meets were held regularly every year. A decade appears short when seen chronologically, but it was sufficiently long enough for kendo to blossom in Canada.

Photo 2-8: First Joint Kendo Taikai (meet) in April 1931, ten years before the Japanese attack on Pearl Harbor. This photo features some of the founders of Canadian kendo.

Photo 2-9: Interestingly, in those days bouts were performed on the stage of the old Japanese Language School, featuring both Japanese and British flags. The sign on the curtain says "*sanbon-shobu*" (best of three points match).

Photo 2-10: Spring Cup Kendo Championship, welcoming Koyama Shihan (head sensei), January 11, 1936

Taken five years after the 1931 photo, the 1936 photo shows twice as many participants. It was taken at a competition commemorating the appointment of Teizo Koyama as the head instructor of Yoshinkan in Vancouver. It was arguably the start of the prewar golden age of kendo in Canada. Incidentally, all these kendo group photos were taken at the same place— the Vancouver Japanese Language School and Japanese Hall. This hall has been remodelled since, but the building remains on Alexander Street near Oppenheimer Park in the Powell Street area of Vancouver. It is still being used today as a Japanese language school among other things. It seems that back in those days, matches were held on the hall's stage.

In 1936, a young Motoo Matsushita, who later taught kendo at the Angler POW Camp, was invited to serve as the head instructor of the Yoshinkan in Vancouver after moving from Wood-fibre, BC. Although he was young, he had undergone proper training in Japan, which was rare in those days in Canada.

Photo 2-11: This photo of the 5th Spring Combined Kendo Championship hosted by Yoshinkan, December 1938, shows that the number of participants had doubled again. The girls in the front row make it clear that women were already practicing kendo before the war.

Photo 2-12: The 6th US–Canada Combined Kendo Championship hosted by Yoshinkan, January 1939. Taken before the outbreak of World War II, the flags of the United Kingdom and Japan are displayed.

Photo 2-12 shows that regular meets between the US and Canada were already taking place. The photo caption says "The 6th" which implies that exchanges between the two countries probably began before or around 1933. In those days, immigrants from Japan were concentrated on the west coast of the North American continent, not just Vancouver, but also Los Angeles, San Francisco and Seattle. Not surprisingly, kendo exchanges between these cities were taking place across the US–Canada border. Because the distance between Vancouver and Seattle is quite

Photo 2-13: Kendo tournament celebrating the *dan* grade promotion of Motoo Matsushita Shihan, November 1940.

short, around 250km, combined championships were frequently held in those days. Joint meets remain common today, but while there are still kendo exchanges between Canada and the US, with the advent of air travel, they are more commonly held within their respective countries.

Sasaburo and his son, Hiromasa Takano, in Prewar Steveston

In 1938, Sasaburo Takano, a well-known Japanese master, leading members of the Waseda University Kendo Club, arrived in the US. It was his second visit there. His ship made a two-day stopover in Vancouver to unload some cargo. Not to miss the great opportunity, the Steveston kenshi asked Takano-sensei to come and teach them.

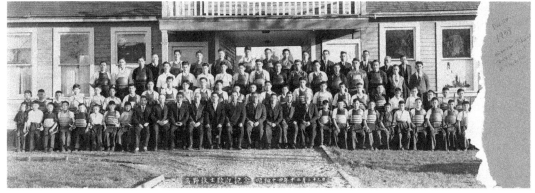

Photo 2-14: An outdoor commemorative group photograph of Hiromasa Takano-sensei's Visit; Steveston, BC in December 1939. The photo commemorates the first and last Canadian Kendo Championship held before the war.

The following year, Sasaburo's second son, Hiromasa Takano, was invited to Steveston to teach. It was during this time that the first and last pre-war Canadian Kendo Championship took place. It was only a nominal Canadian championship as kendo only existed in the province of British Columbia. The winner, Katashi Hibi (1917-2009), recalls that Takano-sensei was the referee for the championship finals. Hibi became an assistant coach at Shoko Dojo in the Angler POW Camp, and would later go on to be a chief editor of book *The Dawning of Pine Lake*, which was discussed in Chapter One.

Photo 2-15: Winners of the 1939 Canadian Kendo Championship. Front row right: Senior champion Katashi Hibi with trophy. The championship trophy in the photo is now in the custody of Nikkei Place, Burnaby, BC. Hibi lived in Thunder Bay after the war, not far from Angler. He passed away at the age of 92. At the time of this photo, he was still a young man of 22. Back row from left: Masao Hayashi, Yuichi Akune and Rintaro Hayashi. Front row from left: Junior champions and brothers, Shigeru and Hiro Niwatsukino.

The high point of Canadian kendo's pre-war golden age was marked by this first championship in 1939. The formation of the Association of Canadian Kendo Dan-Holders took place in 1941, approximately six months before the start of Japan's involvement in World War II in 1941.

About that time, taking a cue from the framed inscription Yoseikan over the entrance in Sasaburo Takano-sensei's own calligraphy, they renamed the Steveston dojo Suchibus-hido Yoseikan (須知武士道養正館). The dojo was the centre of a network that included North Arm, Sunbury, Naka-no-Yado, and several localities in Surrey under its aegis, raising its total membership to 240 members.

This was the Golden Age for kendo in Vancouver, in Steveston, and indeed, in all of Canada. The Association of Canadian Kendo Dan-Holders was formed to foster mutual friendship and liaisons, as well as to hold examinations for *kyu* and *dan* promotions. Its executives comprised:

President: Yuichi Akune
Vice-President: Motoo Matsushita
Director: Eitaro Shoji
Director: Shuzo Tsuruda[3]

The President, Yuichi Akune, was granted 4-dan from the Dai Nippon Butoku Kai (Greater Japan Martial Virtue Society) at the recommendation of Sasaburo Takano-sensei, thereby becoming the leader of kendo in Steveston both by title and in practice.

During this time, baseball, kendo, judo and other cultural activities were undertaken by Japanese immigrants to establish roots in the Japanese community, thanks in large part to the Nisei coming of age.

Rintaro Hayashi mentions that the number of kendo practitioners at the time reached some 240 men across the province, which happens to be not much different from the total kendo population in and around Vancouver today. However, that area of present-day Vancouver only includes Metro Vancouver, and Victoria is much smaller than before the war.

At the time, in addition to Steveston and Vancouver, there were dojo located in North Arm, Sunbury, Surrey, and Haney, where Nikkei farmers lived and worked, and in remote areas such as Ocean Falls and Woodfibre. In comparison, the total kendo population in Canada in 2016 was about 900, of which around 250 were in Metro Vancouver and Victoria. Before the war, all kendo practitioners were Japanese Canadian. Today, that number is probably only 10 or 20 percent.

Continued Passion for Kendo During the War

Through the writings of Rintaro Hayashi, I have explored the history of kendo in the pre-war years. Fortunately, there are many photos in the collections at the Nikkei National Museum in Burnaby, BC that verify his accounts.

---

3   Hayashi Rintaro, *Kanada no kendo ryakushi*, p.4.

As already noted in the previous chapter, Canadian kendo during and after the war was forcibly transplanted to remote locations far from its original birthplaces of Vancouver and Steveston. This demonstrates the burning passion in those who kept up practice, even through years of hardships.

CHAPTER THREE

The Postwar Period

Although postwar kendo in Canada can be subdivided into four periods, it is difficult to clearly define them as they overlap to some degree.

The first period is from immediately after the war to the early 1950s. Apart from two clubs that carried on after the war, kendo did not resume in any significant organized fashion until the early-1950s.

The second period stretched from the early-1950s to the early-1970s. Even though Japanese Canadians were finally allowed to return to the West Coast in 1949, it took several years for kendo to re-establish itself on the coast and spread across the country. The postwar period marked a time when Japanese Canadians were working to get back on their feet and start their lives over, leaving little time for recreational activities. Eventually, a number of those who had been practicing kendo prewar resumed practicing kendo in Steveston. In Vancouver, several of the Shoko Kenshi from the Angler POW camp established the Vancouver Kendo Club. During the same period, two clubs were formed in Toronto, Ontario. The launching of the Canadian Kendo Federation took place in 1966.

During the third period from the 1970s to 2000, young immigrants from Japan, who came on their own initiative or were invited, began to lead kendo alongside the Canadian kendo pioneers. During this period, kendo started to gain recognition among Canadians in general, and spread among the wider population.

Finally, in the fourth period, which began around the year 2000, kendo was led and taught by homegrown Canadian kenshi, mostly Canadian-born Nisei and Sansei (third generation), but also including non-Japanese as well. Many Korean and Chinese Canadians, as well as those from other backgrounds, began to get involved in the Canadian kendo community during this time. For more information on this period, please refer to Appendix 1.

End of the War—Early-1950s

There were two clubs which started during the war and continued to practice after it ended.

Shoko Kenshi in Moose Jaw, Saskatchewan

As indicated in the following photos, Motoo Matasushita and his students practiced kendo in Moose Jaw, Saskatchewan at some point after the war. It seems some of the Shoko Kenshi who chose to go to Japan after the war or did not relocate to cities in the East, were temporarily moved to an Air Force base outside Moose Jaw. There, Shoko Kenshi, who must have carried *bogu* with them during the turbulent postwar period, amazingly continued to practice kendo. It appears that they stayed there for a couple of months, before dispersing across the country or back to Japan.

Photo 3-1: Shoko Kenshi practicing kendo *kata* with bare feet. Matsushita-sensei is facing the camera.

Photo 3-2: Shoko Kenshi practicing *kata* with *bogu*.

Photo 3-3: Shoko Kenshi practicing *kata* with *bogu*.

Yoseikan Kendo Club in Raymond, Alberta 1943–1952

As detailed in Chapter One, the Yoseikan Kendo Club in Raymond started its activities during the war and continued under Yuichi Akune's instruction until 1952, when he returned to Steveston and the club ceased operation.

Yuichi Akune was later recognized on the City of Richmond Wall of Fame for his life-long contribution to kendo. Under his instruction, many young kenshi were trained before, during, and after the war. Over time, a number of them went on to become kendo leaders across Canada in places like Calgary, Manitoba, and even Montreal.

The postwar resumption of kendo in Canada occurred much later than in other countries and regions with established kendo clubs such as the U.S., Hawaii, and Brazil.

It was not until March 1949, over three years after the war ended, that Japanese Canadians were given full citizenship, the right to vote, and freedom of movement. By comparison, in the U.S., which had interned Japanese Americans, the release from the camps began roughly six months before the end of the war, with no restrictions on where they could live.

Canada's postwar policy of forcing Japanese Canadians to move east of the Rocky Mountains or to Japan, a country which many Canadian-born Nisei had never even seen, meant families and individuals were made to choose between the two countries. In the end, over 4,000 Japanese Canadians were deported to Japan, although many would later return.

Those who chose to stay in Canada dispersed across the country, mostly to Ontario and Quebec, but also to the Prairie Provinces. As a result of this demographic shift, kendo, which had been confined largely to British Columbia, spread to the urban centres of eastern Canada including Winnipeg, Manitoba; Toronto, Ontario; and Montreal, Quebec, an unintentional result of the wartime uprooting. Many of those who used to practice in Steveston or Vancouver before the war, along with some Shoko Kenshi from Angler, settled down in these new homes and took up kendo there. There were also those who returned to Canada after being sent to Japan (known as *kika*, or returnees) who took part in kendo activities in various parts of Canada after the war. During this time, Canadian kendo was still led by sensei who were active prewar and/or in the Angler POW Camp during the war. This period of distribution lasted until the mid-1970s. In addition, the majority of the leadership during this period were still in the hands of prewar practitioners.

Photo 3-4: Raymond Kendo Club; Raymond, Alberta, pre-1952. Right of centre is head instructor Yuichi Akune, and to his left is Moriharu Tanigami, who later succeeded Akune at the Steveston Kendo Club.

Early-1950s—Early-1970s

Five major clubs were formed during this key developmental period in postwar Canadian kendo.

Steveston Kendo Club, British Columbia

It was in Steveston, the birthplace of kendo in Canada, where kendo first resumed following the war. Beginning in 1949, former internees started returning to the coast, among them, fishermen who were lured back by the promise of resuming their livelihoods on the water.

Kendo began to take root again rather sporadically among the old and familiar faces from the prewar days. Those who returned were forced to start over from scratch as they had lost everything that they had built up over the years leading up to the war.

With Yuichi Akune's return in 1952 and Rintaro Hayashi's co-management, the club was able to begin to flourish once again. Akune resumed his prewar role as head instructor.

Photo 3-5: Rintaro Hayashi (right) with Yuichi Akune. The two men built kendo's foundation before and after the war in Steveston. Taken at Lemon Creek, BC during the war.

Rintaro Hayashi describes what kendo activity was like at that time:

> With the end of the war, the relocation sites were disbanded. Some kenshi returned to Steveston to resume kendo activities but were not successful at all. Soon Yuichi Akune also returned and, thanks to the kindness of people at the Municipal Hall, we have been able to practice for the past seven years, with the collaboration of Masao Hayashi, Moriharu Tanigami, Takeo Matsubara, Eikichi Matsumura, Yoshiaki Konishi, the Shigeaki brothers, and Susumu Ikuta.[1]

In 1972, the Steveston Martial Arts Centre opened. As Canada's only *budokan* (martial arts centre) it has both a kendo and judo dojo. The centre was built with the support of the city of Richmond and the Steveston community.

Photo 3-6: Steveston Kendo Club in 1966. Third row, fifth from left is Yuichi Akune, main sensei for the Steveston club, and to his left is Torao Mori, visiting from Los Angeles. Second from right is Rintaro Hayashi.

Photo 3-7: Vancouver kendo club in 1973.

---

1   Hayashi Rintaro, *Kanada no kendo ryakushi*, p.4.

Vancouver Kendo Club, British Columbia

The Vancouver Kendo Club formed in 1964, with the Shoko Kenshi from Angler as the core of its group. Participants included Misaho Noda, Shigeru Kuwabara, Kaoru Kimoto, Takeji Yoshimaru, Masanobu Kawahira and Hayaru Koyama, along with Eiji Omae, who was not at Angler. They began practicing in the hall of the Vancouver Buddhist Temple but later relocated to the Renfrew Community Centre. This club, along with the Steveston Kendo Club, has made a huge contribution to the kendo community in Western Canada that continues up to the present day.

Manitoba Kendo Club

Another kendo club was formed in Winnipeg, Manitoba, around 1966, according to the memoirs of Tom Yamashita, a Nisei who is today the key person at the club. He says he began kendo at age 14. The club's leaders were Ichiro Hirayama, Risuke Hamade, Tsuneharu Amadatsu, Masao Hiraoka, and, later, Tatsuo Onodera. They were all kenshi who used to practice kendo in Steveston or Vancouver before the war. Yamashita recalls that when Hamade-sensei was over 70, he was still lugging his *bogu* bag some five kilometres to and from the dojo in Winnipeg. In 1974, the 2nd Canadian Kendo Championship took place in Winnipeg.

Photo 3-8: Founders of the Manitoba Kendo Club. From left: Tatsuo Onodera, Risuke Hamade, Ichiro Hirayama, Tsuneharu Amadate, and Masao Hiraoka. They are mostly from Steveston and the connection between this club and the Steveston club remains strong to this day.

Japanese Canadian Cultural Centre Kendo Club, Ontario

Kaname Asa initially started a practice group at his private company location. Later, after the arrival of two young instructors from Japan, Morito Tsumura and Koki Ariga, they established a kendo club at the Japanese Canadian Cultural Centre (JCCC) in Toronto. In February 1965, a ceremony was held in Toronto to mark the inauguration of the JCCC Kendo Club. On that occasion, Hiromasa Takano, who was visiting Steveston at the time, travelled to Toronto to attend and cut the ceremonial ribbon as well as to give lectures. He was accompanied from

J.C. Cultural Centre Dojo Opened With Sword Cut

TORONTO. — Cutting the ribbon to officially open the Japanese Canadian Cultural Centre's Kendo Dojo is Master Hiromasa Takano, 10th-dan. Holding the ribbon taunt is (left) Mr. Frank Asano, 5th-dan, head of the Centre kendo and (right) Mr. Y. Kimura. Kendo lessons are held on Tuesday and Thursday nights at the J.C. Cultural Centre. Membership is open to men, women and children.

Photo 3-9: Hiromasa Takano cuts the tape with a sword at the inauguration of JCCC Kendo Club. The occasion was carried in the Nikkei newspaper *Tairiku Nippo*.

Vancouver by Rintaro Hayashi and Yuichi Akune for the occasion. A year later, Torao Mori, an outstanding kendoka of international fame, visited Toronto from the US. I will examine Mori in detail in the next chapter. In 1972, an additional two young instructors, Shigetaka Kamata and Kiyoshi Hao, arrived as immigrants and joined JCCC.

Toka Budokan, Ontario

This Toronto-based club was founded around 1964 by Masao Larry Nakamura (1922–2013, born in Vancouver). After leaving the Canadian Kendo Federation, he joined the Nihon Kendo Dojo Renmei (Japanese Kendo Dojo Association) to continue practising kendo at his own dojo. Nakamura energetically devoted his life to what might be called his "kendo diplomacy" by frequently inviting many kendo sensei to Canada from Japan or going himself to Japan for visits and tours with his students. He invited two young instructors from Japan to join his club, Masatoshi Tagawa in 1971 and Shigeo Kimura in 1973. Both migrated to Canada upon graduating from university in Japan.

Photo 3-10: Masao Larry Nakamura, Toka Budokan founder.

Inauguration of the Canadian Kendo Federation (CKF) in 1966

The Canadian Kendo Federation was formed in 1966 by the five kendo clubs and inaugurated at the JCCC Kendo Club in eastern Toronto. The members were listed in Rintaro Hayashi's *Kanada no kendo ryakushi*:

Officers	President	Yuichi Akune
	Vice-President	Masao Nakamura
	Vice-President	Kanzaburo Kobayashi
	Secretary	Yoshikazu Kimura
	Directors	Rintaro Hayashi
		Kaname Asa
		Misaho Noda

These members were from the group of clubs based in Vancouver and Toronto that were established after the war.

Here is a chronology comparing the establishment of kendo federations after the war in the major kendo-practicing nations.

1945   End of the war. Nikkei people in Canada are forced to choose between relocating east of the Rockies or being deported to Japan.

1949   Nikkei people in Canada are allowed to return to the West Coast.

1952   The All Japan Kendo Federation is established.

1953   GHQ (Allied occupation forces) lifts its ban on kendo in Japan.

1955   The U.S. and Hawaiian kendo federations are established.

1959   The Brazilian Kendo Federation is established.

1966   The Canada Kendo Federation is established.

As you can see, the CKF was formed more than 10 years after its neighbouring U.S. kendo federation. This was due to Canada's postwar policy directed towards Japanese Canadians, which intended to stop them from returning to the West Coast.

Arrival of New Kendo Immigrants

At the end of this first period, JCCC and Toka Budokan in Ontario were led by young new immigrants from Japan, bringing a fresh wind to the Canadian kendo community. The seeds that were sown in those days after the war eventually bore fruit, making Toronto one of the two major centres of kendo in Canada, on par with Vancouver. The addition of young Japanese immigrants joining and founding new clubs would continue in the next period across the rest of Canada. These erstwhile young leaders are now all in their late 60s to 70s. In many dojos, the disciples they once trained have themselves become sensei and are actively involved in training new students.

Photo 3-11: Torao Mori (centre) with Kaname Asa (right) and Rintaro Hayashi (left) at Niagara Falls on the Canadian side in 1966.

Photo 3-12: In 1973, the WKC team competition was held in Los Angeles, USA, with Team Canada placing second. Back row from left: Masao Hayashi, Misaho Noda (then CKF president), Yukio Ara, Shigetaka Kamata, Yuichi Akune (CKF first president) and Moriharu Tanigami. Front row from left: Makio Ogawa, Koki Ariga, Morito Tsumura.

Photo 3-13: JCCC Kendo Club's new young immigrant leaders in Toronto.
Second row from left: R. Asa, S. Kamata, K. Ariga, Kaname Asa, M. Noda, M. Tsumura, K. Hao. Photo circa 1978, while Misaho Noda was serving as CKF president.

1974 to 2000

Between 1974–2000, many new kendo clubs sprang up across the country. In this section, I will look at these new clubs along with the existing ones that entered new phases in their development. In this section, I will also discuss dojo in the provinces moving from west to east. See table in Appendix 1.

British Columbia

In 1990, Ray Murao, a Sansei raised in the Steveston Kendo Club succeeded Moriharu Tanigami as the chief instructor, and continues serving to this day. Murao competed in the World Kendo Championships several times and later became the manager of Team Canada. This dojo holds the annual Steveston Kendo Tournament, which continues to be one of the biggest kendo events in North America.

Photo 3-14: Steveston Kendo Club, 1985. Front row from left (only adults): R. Murao, T. Matsubara, M. Tanigami, H. Niwatsukino, K. Ikuta.

During the tenure of Misaho Noda (1917–1992) as its president, Vancouver Kendo Club invited many kendoka from Japan and sponsored an exchange programme between Japanese and Canadian kendo youth. Also, during this period Hirotaka (Yukio) Ara joined the teaching staff for several years before forming his own club, Renbu. After Ara's departure, Akira Hayashi (1949–2008) immigrated to Canada as a young man in 1980 and immediately began practicing with the Vancouver Kendo Club. He joined the teaching staff, which was made up of Angler kenshi, and looked after the children. Later, he took over the position of head instructor, but unfortunately passed away at the young age of 60. Many female players who studied under him successfully participated in the World Kendo Championships (WKC) later on. The club holds an annual kendo championship just like the Steveston Kendo Club.

Photo 3-15: Vancouver Kendo Club, 1985. Second row from left, Mark Noda, Akira Hayashi, Misaho Noda, T. Kurasawa (Japan), Eiji Omae, Masanobu Kawahara.

Renbu Dojo, formed in 1977 by Hirotaka (Yukio) Ara after he left the Vancouver Kendo Club, has played a key role in the development of kendo in Western Canada. Between 1978 and 1982, a number of young kenshi joined this club, some going on to become leaders themselves. Two such people were Hirokazu Okusa and Ted Davis (1946–2007). Okusa immigrated to Canada in 1974 and practiced kendo at Toka Budokan in Toronto before moving to Vancouver. Ted Davis, originally from Portland, Oregon, was assisted by Ara in his kendo and iaido studies through personal introductions in Japan.

Okusa formed the University of British Columbia Kendo Club in 1978, pioneering collegiate kendo in British Columbia. Ted Davis opened the University of Victoria Kendo Club the following year. In 2000, Okusa left the UBC Kendo Club and started the Simon Fraser University Kendo Club. These three university clubs started an intercollegiate tournament in 2006.

Ara also invited a few young kendoka from Japan as visitors. Among them were Mitsuru Asaoka (1945-2019) and Ken Miyaoka who both later immigrated to Canada. In 1981, Asaoka opened the Sunrise Kendo Club with Takuo Uegaki, another immigrant. This club would result in three clubs: the Sunrise Kendo Club, continued by Uegaki; Yoshinkan, led by Asaoka; and the Renfrew Kendo Club, led by another immigrant, Yoshiaki Taguchi. That same year, Ken Miyaoka relocated to Saskatoon, Saskatchewan and opened his own club.

With the exception of Ted Davis and Ray Murao, these core leaders in western Canada are all new immigrants from Japan. This wave of new immigrant leaders established themselves in Western Canada almost ten years after the same phenomenon occurred in Ontario.

Alberta

The Calgary Kendo Club was established at Mount Royal College by Susumu Ikuta (1926–2016) in 1974. As mentioned earlier, Ikuta began studying kendo at age 14, first under Yuichi Akune during the war years in Raymond, Alberta, where the family had been relocated.

Saskatchewan

As previously noted, Ken Miyaoka, a former member of Renbu Dojo, moved to Saskatoon, Saskatchewan, in 1981 and launched the Saskatoon Kendo Club. It is today the nucleus of kendo in the Canadian Prairies. He was truly a pioneer in the hinterlands of kendo. A kendo club has since been formed in Regina, providing the province with its second kendo club.

Photo 3-16: A Saskatoon seminar in 2016 was a resounding success. The man at the center of the front row is Morito Tsumura with Ken Miyaoka on his left and Hirokazu Okusa to his right. To Miyaoka's left is Neil Gendzwill, who serves as CKF secretary.

Manitoba

The Manitoba Kendo Club, located in Winnipeg, has been continued by Tom Yamashita who learned kendo in this dojo and is the current sensei.

Ontario

Ontario today boasts the largest kendo population of all the provinces in Canada partly due to the infusion of young instructors from Japan in the seventies and earlier. This introduction of new energetic power helped make kendo very popular in Eastern Canada.

The Etobicoke Olympium Kendo & Iaido Club was founded in 1980 in a western suburb of Toronto as a sister dojo to the JCCC Kendo Club by former JCCC instructors Koki Ariga and Shigetaka Kamata. David Johnson, with head instructor Morito Tsumura, formed the University of Toronto Kendo Club in 1977. Shigeo Kimura, who became independent from

Toka Budokan, started kendo training under the name Takubukan around 1978. The name was later changed to Toronto Kendo Club. The University of Waterloo Kendo Club was opened by Taro Ariga under Shigetaka Kamata in 1987. In Canada's capital, Ottawa, Ontario, the Ottawa Kendo Club, Tateyama Dojo and the Carlton University Kendo Club are among those operating at the time of writing.

Quebec

Montreal, the largest city in the French-speaking province of Quebec in Eastern Canada, has become one of the three major driving forces in Canadian kendo after Vancouver and Toronto .

The pioneers of kendo in Montreal were two men, Douglas Funamoto (1914–2001) and Kiyoshi Ono (1918–2004). Funamoto came from Japan at age 16 and learned kendo from age 20 at Yoshinkan in Vancouver under Atsumu Kamino and Teizo Koyama, as mentioned in Chapter Two. He served as Koyama's assistant until the start of war. He recalled that in 1936 he had a chance to practice with well-known kendoka Sasaburo Takano in Vancouver when the latter made a stopover on his way to Los Angeles as leader of the Waseda University Kendo Club. He met Hiromasa Takano as well in 1938, which was before the war. After the war, he moved to Montreal.

Kiyoshi Ono was born in Canada but was sent to Japan as a child, where he started kendo at his primary school in Odawara, Kanagawa prefecture. In 1938 he returned to Canada and went to work in Ocean Falls in British Columbia's hinterland. As there was a kendo club there, it is possible that he continued to practice kendo there, too. Thereafter, he was sent to the Angler POW camp where he kept up kendo as one of the Shoko Kenshi. He moved to Montreal after the war. Ono and Funamoto practiced and taught together at Immaculee-Conception Dojo de Montreal.

Later in 1978, Ono formed the Montreal Kendo Club, which was succeeded by Junko Ariyama, and Funamoto also opened Shidokan and was succeeded by Santoso Hanitijo. The Quebec Kendo Club was founded by Hiroshi Awaga in 1986 in Quebec City, the provincial capital. In 1990, Christian D'Orangeville established McGill University Kendo Club in Montreal. He succeeded Hirokazu Okusa as president of the Canadian Kendo Federation in 2014. Gilles Valiquette's Isshinkai Kendo Club also opened in 1991 in Montreal.

Photo 3-17: In 2006 at the 13th WKC in Taiwan, Team Canada Women's Team achieved third place. Back row from left: Roy Asa (CKF President), Ray Murao (Coach), Chiharu Hao, Makiko Hayashi, Akiko Fukushima, Brian Asa (Assistant Manager), Manabu Ogawa (Trainer). Front row from left: Natsuko Fukushima, Wendy Robillard (Coach), Shiho Kamata, Yuki Hayashi, Maya Taguchi.

After 2000

The more recent history is too close to be captured in detail objectively. Hopefully, in the future someone will write a Canadian kendo history covering the years after 2000. However, I would like to describe a general trend and one kendo milestone. After 2000, some of the students that were trained under the instructors mentioned in the previous periods became sensei themselves and either took over as head instructors of existing clubs or started new clubs. These new instructors were Canadian-born Nisei and Sansei, as well as people of non-Japanese backgrounds. This is a significant development that illustrates how kendo has sprouted new roots in Canada.

Another sign of new roots is the increase in university and college clubs with over ten across the country. Due to the vast distances separating East and West, separate intercollegiate kendo championships have been held since 2006. The first all-Canada intercollegiate was held in 2008 in Toronto.

Canadian Kendo Federation Officers

From the establishment of the Canadian Kendo Federation (CKF) to the present day, the make-up of the officers has changed significantly from only those of Japanese origin to a more ethnically-diverse composition, which reflects Canada's pluralistic society. One significant example is that the former president is originally from France. Here is a list of former federation presidents.

- Yuichi Akune (BC), the first CKF president, served 1966–1971.
- Misaho Noda (BC) served 1971–1980. A founding member of the federation in 1966, he led young kenshi, both boys and girls, to Japan and in turn invited well-known kendoka from Japan to visit Canada.
- Roy Tadayoshi Asa (Ontario) served for 29 years, from 1980–2009. During this extended period, the foundation of Canadian kendo was established, especially its finances and the grading system across the country. He actively organized the Canadian National Championships. During this time, he also served as a Vice President of the International Kendo Federation, which elevated Canada's position internationally.
- Hirokazu Okusa (BC) served from 2009–2014, during which time the board registered as a new society with the government, established a new set of by-laws and made some reforms in the finances of the federation.
- Christian D'Orangeville (Quebec) has served from 2014 to the present (as of 2020). Since he was originally a European and resides in Eastern Canada, he has a strong connection with the European Kendo Federation. He also serves as a member of the anti-doping committee of the International Kendo Federation (FIK).

Photo 3-18: Roy Asa (front row, second from right) awarded for his long-time dedication as a vice president of the International Kendo Federation (FIK) by the All Japan Kendo Federation in 2010. Centre right is the former president of the AJKF, Yoshimitsu Takeyasu.

Of note, John Maisonneuve has served for two terms as treasurer from 2009 to the present. Neil Gendzwill has served as long-time secretary and is actively involved in the day-to-day activities of the CKF. Refer to Appendix 2 for changes in Canadian Kendo Federation officers and major events for examples of how the makeup of the officers has changed.

Photo 3-19: From left, John Maisonneuve (long-time CKF treasurer), Hirokazu Okusa (former president) and Christian D'Orangeville (CKF president, as of 2020).

Photo 3-20: Neil Gendzwill, long-time secretary of the CKF.

Photo 3-21: CKF officials in 2012. Front row, from left: Shigetaka Kamata (National grading chief), Hirokazu Okusa (then-president), Ray Murao (Team Canada manager), Shigeo Kimura and Yoshiaki Taguchi (WKC official shinpan). Second row, first left: Daisuke Hayashi (Team Canada Women's coach). Fourth row, first left: Mathew Raymond (Team Canada Men's coach).

Recent Development

Kendo clubs or dojo rarely start out in complete isolation. Most of them develop the way cells multiply. Usually, sensei and their disciples separate and branch out to form new dojos. In that respect kendo is a small world, even in the vast terrain of Canada.

Taking a bird's-eye view of the over-100-year-old history of kendo in Canada, it is like slow-growing roots that germinated on the West Coast and then spread slowly but surely over time across the country.

The Japanese people's strong sense of identity and the universality of their culture can be observed through kendo. Inheritance or propagation of culture seems to be much stronger when it is compressed and condensed into a certain form or container, like kendo, rather than when it is simply passed on to descendants. But it is also inevitable that the shape of the container itself would be affected by the locality where the people to whom it is passed on to live, and that it reflects changes that cannot be avoided.

In Canada, the make-up of participants in the World Kendo Championship, which used to consist exclusively of Nikkei, has changed significantly over the years, as have the officers who are managing the Canadian Kendo Federation. Christian D'Orangeville, who succeeded me as CKF president, resides in Montreal, and is not Nikkei. He was a fencer in his native France but was captivated by kendo when he visited Japan. His passion for kendo is no less than that of Nikkei practitioners. This is evidence that the seeds sown by the Nikkei pioneers have taken root over the past 100 years, and that the branches and leaves have spread mightily. As Japanese migration to Canada has slowed down considerably in recent decades, the future of Canadian kendo is now in the hands of Canadians of all backgrounds.

Photo 3-22: Poster for the 17th championship in Vancouver, marking the centenary of kendo in Canada.

CHAPTER FOUR

Motoo Matsushita and Torao "Tiger" Mori
—Two Kendoka Across the Pacific—

The previous chapters introduced Motoo Matsushita and his activities during the prewar and war years. I will now look at his kendo career in more detail, particularly his life in Japan after the war. I will also look at Torao "Tiger" Mori, a well-known kendo figure and fencer who was very active in kendo in prewar Japan and the US, and who played a major role in the establishment of the World Kendo Championships.

I will trace the passion for kendo that ran through these two men, who were born in the same period but in different countries separated by the Pacific Ocean. By studying these two kendoka's lives, it is possible to see how kendo developed in North America during their time there, and how the war impacted kendo and their lives.

Photo 4-1: Motoo Matsushita, representing Gunma prefecture.

Hereafter, I will refer to them by their first names as a way of showing affection. Most of the information and photos concerning Torao are sourced from Toshiyuki Hayase's book *Taigaa Mori to Yobareta Otoko* (The Man They Called Tiger Mori). This chapter would not have been possible without the benefit of this great literary effort, driven by Hayase's passion for researching Torao's life. I would like to express my gratitude for the author's permission to use his book as a primary and dependable source. I also acknowledge several Torao Mori websites that provided information on his activities in the US. I was also fortunate to acquire and use a booklet, *Suen Kenyu* (an edition of the Sugamo Gakuen kendo society's published in memory of Torao Mori), which was issued three months after his sudden death.

Photo 4-2: Torao Mori.

Canadian-born Motoo (1918 – 1991)

Motoo was born in 1918 in Britannia Beach, British Columbia, approximately an hour's drive from Vancouver. Britannia Beach was best known as having Canada's biggest copper mine in the 1900s. I assume his father worked for the mine. There was a settlement of Japanese workers here, known to the locals as "Japtown", an indication of the casual racism that was prevalent at the time.

Moving to Japan

In those days, it was a common practice among Japanese immigrants in Canada to send their children to Japan when they reached primary school-age to attend school there. They would receive a Japanese education under the guardianship of grandparents, relatives or acquaintances. Their parents would send money from Canada to cover expenses. Most of the early immigrants considered themselves to be "*dekasegi*" (people who came to earn money) and many felt that their children should be raised as Japanese. Most of the children would then return to Canada after graduating from primary or secondary school to re-join their parents.

Motoo was one such child who was sent to Japan for schooling. He started kendo in the fifth grade there, and he must have been talented because it is recorded that he was a runner-up in the boys' division of the Meiji Jingu Taiiku Taikai (Meiji Shrine Athletic Meet) when he was only in the sixth grade.

He went on to attend Maebashi Commercial High School, where he became a member of the kendo club. Thereafter he trained for three months at Meishinkan Takano Dojo (the predecessor of Shudo Gakuin), one of the most well-known dojo in Tokyo at the time.

Returning to Canada

Motoo returned to Canada in 1936 when he was 19 years old. The first job he found was at a pulp production plant in Woodfibre, a remote settlement of 300 to 400 Nikkei workers who either had families or were single and lived in bunkhouses.

At that time in Canada, kendo had already entered its prewar golden era as discussed in Chapter Two. Kendo and judo were popular among Japanese immigrants as a means of inculcating traditional Japanese values and manners in their children. The foundations for the kendo community were thus laid by immigrants from Japan.

His return was just five years before Japan and Canada went to war, so these were turbulent times to say the least. There was extreme racial discrimination in Canada, especially in British Columbia, as well as mounting antagonism toward Japan over its entry into Manchuria. Motoo started teaching kendo in Woodfibre before moving to Vancouver where he worked in the Powell Street neighbourhood. In Vancouver, he was invited to become the head instructor at Yoshinkan, which had been established in 1923. He went on to earn promotion to 4-dan in 1940, four years after his return and one year before Japan entered World War II.

Photo 4-3: Top photo caption: Competition to celebrate Matsushita sensei's promotion (November 1940). Motoo Matsushita in black suit at the centre of 2nd row. To his right is Rintaro Hayashi.

Wartime

During the war, Motoo was sent to POW Camp #101 in Angler, Ontario, where he kept practicing and teaching kendo at Shoko Dojo as discussed in Chapter One.

Postwar

In May 1946, a year after the war ended, Japanese Canadians were given two choices: be "repatriated" to Japan or relocate east of the Rockies. Motoo chose to go back to Japan rather than remain in Canada. He was age 28 when he returned to Japan with his younger brother Shigeo Matsushita amidst the chaos that followed Japan's defeat. In the aftermath of the war, life in Japan was hard, but it must have been even more so for those like Motoo and Shigeo who were used to life in Canada and were forced to readjust and make a fresh start.

After returning to Japan, Motoo took close to ten years

Photo 4-4: Motoo as the Shoko Kenshi's sensei at Angler POW Camp.

to settle down before becoming very active in kendo. From his late thirties to early fifties, he participated in numerous official tournaments, representing Gunma prefecture, his second home. At some point, he opened a private dojo to teach the locals in Maebashi, Gunma. The dojo was called Shokokan, which I believe must have been named after Shoko Dojo in Angler.

Motoo's Kendo Tournament Record in Japan

Motoo participated in many matches following his return to Japan. Below are those I found in the archives of the All Japan Kendo Federation.

In 1955, nine years after his return, he entered the 5th Nikko Kendo Competition and won first place in the 6- and 7-dan category at age 37. The 1st Nikko Kendo Competition, held in 1951, along with the Peace Treaty Commemoration National Goodwill Kendo Competition held in 1952, were considered to be the womb from which the postwar All Japan Kendo Federation was born.[1] This competition was a major one at the national level at the time.

The same year, he also entered the 3rd Todofuken Taikai (All Japan Inter-prefecture Kendo Championship), in which he participated a further eight more times. In these championships he was named Fukusho (vice-captain) eight times and Taisho (captain) for Gunma prefecture once. The last time he participated was in 1970 at age 52.

Photo 4-6: Motoo visited Vancouver on his first trip to Canada after the war to reunite with the Shoko Kenshi (sensei of the Vancouver Kendo Club) in 1967. He later visited Vancouver on two more occasions.

---

1   Hanazono Mitsunori, *Kendo no Fukkatsu*, p. 269.

Motoo also entered the All Japan Kendo Championship four times. The first time was in the seventh edition, held in 1959 when he was 41. That year Motoo lost in the second round to Taro Nakamura, who went on to become champion. He competed again in 1961 and 1962, with his final appearance in 1965 in the 13th championship at the age of 47.

Photo 4-7: After Vancouver, Motoo visited Toronto, where he had a reunion with the Shoko Kenshi. Front row: Yoshikazu Kimura, Rintaro Hayashi, Motoo Matsushita, Kaname Asa, Dick Tsuruda. Back row: Masatoshi Okazaki (older brother), Katsumasa Okazaki (younger brother), George Kumagai (older brother), Seiko Kumagai (younger brother) Tomio Sameshima, Koichi Kawamoto, unknown.

Motoo's Character

Motoo was by all accounts a likable and humble man. A comment by Rintaro Hayashi about a prewar conversation between the two men captures Motoo's character:

> …The first time I met Mr. Matsushita was when I went to a kendo competition. In the car on the way, he shared with me recollections of the matches he fought in his student days, but not a single one about beating an opponent. I cannot remember his opponent's name, but this is how the conversation went.
>
> "It was really great that time. As soon as I thought his *shinai* went up, it came down and 'smack!'"
>
> "So you got his *kote*?"
>
> "No, he got ME!"
>
> At the time, Mr. Matsushita was around 22 or 23, so he was about my son's age, and I liked him because he was not at all conceited.[2]

---

2   Hayashi Rintaro, *Kouhan Mandan*, p.131.

There are many words of gratitude dedicated to Motoo from his pupils in *Akeyuku Shoko* .

Japanese-born Torao (1914–1969)

Torao Mori was born Torao Noma in Kiryu, Gunma prefecture, in 1914. Kiryu was a major silk-producing town since the Meiji era and contributed significantly to the Japanese economy. Torao's family was involved in the silk business. In 1922, when he was eight years old, he was adopted by his uncle Seiji Noma, founder of the major publishing house, Kodansha, in Tokyo. There, while still a boy, he received training at Noma Dojo, together with Seiji's only son, Hisashi, under the tutelage of first-rate instructors including Moriji Mochida, Shinsuke Masuda, and Giichi Abe, a disciple of Hakudo Nakayama. Noma Dojo was established three years after Torao's arrival in Tokyo.

Photo 4-8: Torao (centre) at Noma Dojo, Tokyo, high school age, with Hiromichi (Hakudo) Nakayama to his right.

Torao went on to join the kendo club of Sugamo Commercial High School, which had a very strong kendo programme, and started to practice there, as well as at Noma Dojo. For the time, he was extraordinarily progressive in his many interests, taking up photography and ballroom dancing as hobbies. His attentiveness, sixth sense, nimbleness, and freedom of movement were all qualities that contributed to his later success in fencing in the U.S.

In the years to come, every kendoka who saw Torao's kendo would, without exception, praise the elegance and beauty of his movements. From the start, he received the highest standard training reserved for the elites by the "cream of the crop" of instructors. This, in addition to his natural-born talent, led him to win three national middle school kendo championships from 1929 to 1931, indicating his talent had already fully bloomed by then. His match three years later against Hisashi Noma in the finals of the traditional *tenran-jiai* (matches conducted in front of the Emperor), which he lost, would be talked about for years.

Torao changed his surname from Noma to Mori in 1929. A man named Yozo Mori was one of the "Big Four" at Chiba Dojo during the Edo period (1603–1868). He later served under the Iino Clan, a branch of the Aizu Clan, and in 1868 died in the Boshin War along with his son Torao[3] in a hail of enemy bullets. His eldest daughter Fuyu was Torao Noma's grandmother. In other words, Torao was a great-grandson of Yozo Mori, and as such, it is said that he had to carry on that surname for posterity.

In 1935, Torao joined the Imperial Army at age 21, entering the Maebashi 15th Regiment. In April of that year, he was sent to the front in Manchuria where he was assigned to a tank corps.

Torao visits the United States

Torao traveled to the United States in 1937 at age 22 carrying three *shinai* and *bogu* with a clear mission: promote kendo in the US, particularly Los Angeles. Now an official 5-dan instructor with the Dai-Nippon Butoku Kai (Greater Japan Martial Virtue Society), he was heartily welcomed in Honolulu in January 1937, where he stayed for a month. Then in March he arrived on the US mainland where, again, he was enthusiastically received by local kendo practitioners.

Japanese immigrants in the US continued to practice kendo even as they struggled to secure a livelihood, so there were already a fair number of dojo in the US. Pioneers like Sasaburo Takano (first in 1931, and again in 1938) and Tokichi Nakamura (from 1929–1938) had already spent time promoting kendo and providing instruction in the US. The US West Coast was experiencing the same popularity that Canada was at the time. It can be assumed that as an already well-known figure in the kendo world, Torao must have been active on many fronts.

Torao Takes Up Fencing

Interestingly, Torao took up the western sport of fencing, in which he also became successful in an unusually short time. When Torao left Japan, the Greater Japan Fencing Association

---

3   The pronunciation of the name is the same but it is written with different characters.

asked him to study the sport in preparation for the 1940 Tokyo Olympic Games, which were subsequently cancelled. We can assume he used his kendo experience to facilitate his rapid mastery of the sport. Torao had the good fortune of meeting Professor Henri Uyttenhove, a fencing master from Belgium, at the Los Angeles Athletic Club. Uyttenhove coached Torao to the top of the fencing world. Almost eight months after his arrival, Torao became the champion of the US western region. In April 1938 he entered the national competition held in New York where he reached the finals but lost. Torao's coach objected to the decision, but at the time a human judging system was employed in fencing and it would have been difficult to celebrate a Japanese man becoming the US champion in the prewar environment.

Torao received his nickname, Tiger, due not only to the fact that "Torao" means tiger-man in Japanese, but because his fencing was superb as well. No matter how talented he was, however, he would not have been able to do that well without people supporting him. This is more proof of his good luck and likeable character.

Having become a fencing champion in the Los Angeles area within a year, Torao became a well-known figure and was able to use that fame to further promote kendo. Reading about his life in Hayase's book, I was impressed by his ability to make inroads into high society, including mingling with Hollywood movie stars. He was able to do this even though Japan's military presence in Manchuria had already been established by the time he arrived in the US and a storm of anti-Japanese sentiment was beginning to mount. This was of course due to his ability to handle any situation with his flexibility of mind.

During Torao's stay in the US, he began a relationship with a Japanese American, a Nisei named Janice Teiko Akaboshi, which must have helped him tremendously. From Janice, he must have been able to absorb various aspects of American culture.

Torao returned to Japan after a year and a half in the US, having amassed many kendo disciples and fencing-related acquaintances in that brief time. This would become a big asset for Torao in the years to come, helping him even during the chaotic postwar era in Japan. Apart from a small number of Caucasians like Gordon Warner[4], most kendo practitioners in the US were Japanese or Nisei, whereas his fencing acquaintances were not.

---

4   Gordon Warner visited Japan in 1937 after meeting Torao in LA and receiving a letter of introduction from him. Warner was very active in promoting kendo and iaido after the war. In 1989 he wrote the book *This is Kendo* in English.

After returning to Japan in 1938, Torao taught kendo to officer cadets at the Narashino Education Corps in Chiba. In May of 1940, Janice Akaboshi travelled by herself to Japan, something that would have been uncommon in the social climate just before the war, and the two were married. That August, the couple travelled to Manchuria, returning home by the way of Dalian. Torao was then 26 years old.

Photo 4-9: The wedding of Torao Mori and Janice Teiko Akaboshi in May 1940.

Wartime

In 1942, at the goodwill tournament in Manchuria between kenshi stationed in Manchuria and kenshi from Japan, Torao performed a demonstration *shiai* against his sensei Moriji Mochida. Following the closure of Noma Dojo in 1944, he was not able to practice any more until the next year, when the family was forced to relocate to Kiryu, his birthplace, due to bombing attacks on Tokyo by the U.S. In Kiryu, Torao often visited a nearby dojo, Kokubukan, that was built by Seiji Noma and others before the war, and he quietly trained by himself. His morning custom was to do one thousand *suburi*.

This evacuation was difficult for Torao and Janice on several fronts. Along with their two small children, they lived with his parents and siblings, making it especially difficult for Janice. Additionally, their close connections to the United States meant that they were viewed with suspicion by the locals.

Torao Mori after the War

In the fall of 1946, Torao Mori was still living in Kiryu when he received a visit from Paul Minakami, an American Nisei soldier who had been one of his kendo pupils in the US before the war. On Minakami's advice, he opened a social club for the US occupation forces around that time and managed it until 1950. It would have been of tremendous help to his business that his wife Janice was a US citizen, and that he himself had been a big star in kendo and fencing in the US. In fact, it was so successful that by 1948, he was able to build his own home. Eventually, with the assets he had made from his club business, he moved to America in 1950 where he flourished.

Torao's return re-invigorated the U.S. kendo community and he became a consultant to the Southern California Dan Holder's Association. Torao was elected the first president of the Kendo Federation of the USA (KFUSA, forerunner of the All United States Kendo Federation (AUSKF)) in 1955.

Torao became very active in promoting exchanges between Japanese and US kendo delegations. In November 1956, he formed a youth kendo study group to plan for an upcoming tour of Japan. The group worked out for two weeks in Japan and observed the All Japan Kendo Championship.

He also organized the Japan-US Goodwill Kendo Competition for young kenshi in 1957. A contingent of 13 students selected from throughout Japan, headed by Junzo Sasamori, visited the US.

Photo 4-10: Japan–US Goodwill Kendo Championship in Los Angeles with Torao Mori officiating as referee.

In 1963, Torao again played the role of a bridge spanning Japan and both North and South America in order to further the internationalization of kendo. He organized a kendo goodwill delegation from Japan consisting of Yuji Oasa, Takashi Ozawa, Shinsuke Masuda, Toshio Watanabe, and Kazuto Toshioka. The delegation conducted four demonstrations in Los Angeles and two in Brazil.

Photo 4-11: Members of the mission in LA. (Right to left) Yuji Oasa, Takashi Ozawa, Shinsuke Masuda, Toshio Watanabe, and Kazuto Toshioka.

Photo 4-12: Highest-ranked kendoka Yuji Oasa (third from left) and Torao (second from right) with award winners in Los Angeles.

Photo 4-13: Iaido demonstration by Torao in Los Angeles.

Photo 4-14: An article in *Sanpauro Shinbun* (São Paulo Newspaper). It says that almost 2,000 spectators gathered to watch Tiger Mori and the kendo delegation from Japan.

Photo 4-15: The delegation in São Paulo, Brazil.

Torao: An Outstanding Kendoka

The following words describing Torao's kendo character are by Torataro Nakahara, who became the KFUSA's second president after Torao passed away.

> …I was pretty good in Keijo (present day Seoul, Korea), but until I fought Torao-san, I didn't realize he was that strong. Of all the men I fought, Junichi Haga had been the strongest until then, but thereafter, I thought those two were the truly superior ones….[5]

Also, according to Hanshi 8-dan Masataka Inoue:

> … No matter what, his *zanshin* after striking was beautiful . . . In his stance or in his strikes, he was very elegant. His was the ideal form of a workout, like drawing a picture. It is commonly said that those whose sword strokes are beautiful are weak in real competition. But in his case, his *keiko* form was beautiful and he was also outstandingly strong in competition. Back in the old days, there was some *ashigake* (fighting with foot techniques) too, but he was strong there as well. …[6]

There is another comment about Torao's kendo abilities by Rod Nobuto Omoto (who will be discussed in appendix 6), a friend. He said of himself, "I am a student of Torao's."

> …Torao Mori-sensei is a legendary figure in the worlds of kendo and fencing. His sword stance (*kenpu*) was calm and collected but once he was on the attack, he had perfect control of *jodan* so that he could strike at will with exquisite timing, leaving the opponent helpless, unable to do anything. He was one of a kind.[7]

One of Torao's unique kendo training methods is described in the booklet, *Suen kenyu No.10*, a memorial edition for Torao Mori, published by Sugamo Gakuen Kenyu-kai three months after his death in 1969. This following excerpt is a part of a conversation between Moriji Mochida and Giichi Masuda, both Torao's sensei at Noma Dojo.

> Masuda: What impressed me about his kendo training was that he often watched himself in the mirror placed at the corner of dojo. Before *keiko* or after *keiko*, he always fixed his posture and practiced swinging his *shinai* in front of the mirror. He did it every

---

5   Hayase Toshiyuki, *Taiga Mori to Yobareta Otoko*, p.257.
6   Hayase Toshiyuki, *Taiga mori to yobareta otoko*, p.244.
7   —from the website of Tom Bolling

morning. He corrected his bad habits by himself. This attitude was quite different from other people.

Mochida: Indeed, he really did use a mirror. No one else did it.[8]

Torao's Fencing after the War

Right after the war ended in 1945, kendo was banned by General Headquarters (GHQ) of the Occupation forces in Japan and not reinstated until 1952. As a result, some of Torao's students took up fencing instead. Torao did some private fencing teaching, and also served as vice president of the Japan Fencing Association for a short time from 1948.

Following his return to the US in 1950, Torao resumed his fencing career. He won all his matches in the sabre category in competitions in the West Coast region near LA. "Tiger" Mori was back. Torao energetically started teaching fencing to Americans at different locations including the Rotary Club, University of Southern California and the LA Athletic Center. Consequently, he was appointed as the US Olympic fencing team's coach three times: Rome, Tokyo and Mexico. Notably, Torao was inducted into the International Fencing Federation (FIE) Hall of Fame in 2013.

Satoru Sugo, who was one of Torao's fencing students at Chuo University, noted that Torao played a great role in re-establishing and contributing to the development of fencing in Japan.[9]

Photo 4-16: Torao Mori in fencing gear.

Photo 4-17: Torao Mori taught fencing at Chuo University. Torao (center) and Satoru Sugo (second row, right).

8 Arai Shunichi (ed.), *Suen Kenyu No.10*, p.4.
9 Arai Junichi (ed.), *Suen Kenyu No.10*, p.36.

Even after returning to the US, Torao went back to Japan regularly, where he taught fencing mainly at Meiji University and Chuo University.

Torao in Businesses

Along with kendo and fencing, Torao Mori's successes in business cannot be ignored. He joined Taiyo Securities as a partner in 1954, then launched his own business, Mori Securities. He was active in selling securities, especially Japanese stocks to US investors during the country's postwar high-growth era.

By 1967, however, Torao already knew there was something wrong with his health and he withdrew from the front line of his business. He sold off Mori Securities and set up his fencing academy. The academy was run on a membership basis, with reportedly as many as 100 members at a time. With his natural ability to adapt, Torao was a good networker in American society and became the first Japanese board member of the LA Athletic Association.

Torao's Dream of the World Kendo Championships

In his latter years, Torao was actively involved in kendo and fencing. But his dream remained the realization of a world kendo championships.

He seems to have started out by persuading kendo people in other countries to form their own federations. Toward that end, he travelled often to lay the groundwork. He frequently travelled from his base in LA to Japan, Canada, Brazil and elsewhere. I would like to highlight a conversation from one such trip, taken from a letter that Rintaro Hayashi in Vancouver wrote to Morito Tsumura in Toronto in 1980.

> …Mr. Torao Mori went to Hawaii and said to them "Shouldn't you join the US Kendo Federation because Hawaii is part of the US?" The reply was "What are you talking about, you brat! Kendo in Hawaii has a history older than yours. If you want us to come together that much, you guys should join our federation." This must be true because Mr. Mori told me about it himself…[10]

In Hayashi's unique way of describing the conversation between them, he recreates the atmosphere of that occasion. Even today, Hawaii is a member of the International Kendo Federation as an independent entity from the AUSKF.

---

10   Rintaro Hayashi to Morito Tsumura, April 13, 1980.

Photo 4-18: Steveston, BC, Torao in suit in the centre with many Canadians and sensei from the U.S., who had been invited in 1966.

In 1966, Torao Mori visited Canada at the invitation of the Steveston Kendo Club. After Steveston, he went to Toronto, teaching kendo and taking part in workouts there. He also gave instruction in fencing to some Canadians. As he already had the experience of serving as the US fencing team's coach at the 1960 Rome Olympic Games and the 1964 Tokyo Games, the name Tiger Mori was known internationally in the fencing world.

Rintaro Hayashi, who accompanied him to Toronto, wrote in a letter at the time that Torao wanted the US Kendo Federation to have its own *dan* designation and *shogo*, independent from the All Japan Kendo Federation. He suggested to Rintaro Hayashi that the Canadians do the same. Based on a 1980 letter to Tsumura, it seems Hayashi agreed to go along with the idea.

Photo 4-19: Torao sightseeing at Niagara Falls in 1966, during a visit to Toronto.

The First International Goodwill Kendo Championship

In 1967, Torao's dream was nearing reality. The International Goodwill Kendo Championship was held at the Nippon Budokan, with 11 countries participating. It was at this time that a resolution for the establishment of the International Kendo Federation was passed. This was the precursor to the World Kendo Championships.

Photo 4-20: The closing ceremony of the International Goodwill Kendo Championship.

Photo 4-21: Then-Crown Prince Akihito, Princess Michiko and Prince Hironomiya were in attendance at the International Goodwill Championship in 1967.

The team bouts were held in Tokyo while individual bouts took place in Osaka. At the event in Tokyo, Torao, along with Seiji Mochida, demonstrated the Nippon Kendo Kata, while in Osaka he faced Toshio Watanabe in a demonstration match. However, his heart condition had already deteriorated, so when he took off his *men* after this demonstration, his face was very pale. He was later hospitalized for three days.

Photo 4-22: Special advisers Moriji Mochida (left) and Goro Saimura. Both kendoka held the highest rank then.

Photo 4-23: Torao Mori (left) giving a demonstration with his sensei, Moriji Mochida.

Torao Mori Passes Away

Torao had suffered from heart problems for a number of years. It forced him to gradually withdraw from his businesses. On January 8, 1969, he collapsed and died from a heart attack at age 54 during a kendo practice at his dojo.

Photo 4-24: Canada–U.S. friendship competition in 1969, just a month and a half after Torao passed away. If he had been alive, he would surely have been lining up for this photo. The people in the first two rows are kendo leaders on the west coast of the U.S. and Canada.

The World Kendo Championships that Torao Mori had dreamed of took place at the Nippon Budokan in April 1970, a year after his death, with 128 competitors from 17 nations.

This competition has continued, with the 16th edition returning to the Nippon Budokan in 2015, with over 800 participants from 56 nations and territories in individual and team bouts.

I will quote again the following message written by one Shoko Kenshi from the Angler POW camp over 70 years ago.

> … they (Canadian officers) were also reported to have said they would like to encourage it (kendo) for Canadians. In the not-too-distant future, an era will surely arrive when kendo will take a major leap forward as a world-scale sport.[11]

Who could have imagined that this hope, made by a camp internee, would one day become a reality?

---

11   Angler P.O.W. Camp Shoko Dojo Members, *Akeyuku Shoko*, p.47.

Motoo vs. Torao

Although Motoo and Torao lived through the turbulent years surrounding World War II, they never met, spending their lives dedicated to kendo on their respective shores of the Pacific. After the war, Motoo moved from Canada to Japan, and Torao moved from Japan to the United States.

When Motoo returned to Canada as a young man before the war, he started working at a pulp production plant in a remote location and began teaching kendo. In contrast, Torao Mori landed in Los Angeles before the war, a bustling American metropolis, assigned with a kendo mission and carrying a letter of accreditation from the Japanese kendo authority. As a well-known figure, he was welcomed by kendo practitioners in the US and was able to build on the foundations they had established using a capability and personality that enabled him to thrive. Clearly there was a significant difference in the environments the two men found themselves in.

To use a metaphor for these two kendoka in terms of woven cloth, Motoo Matsushita's life was like cotton: plain and simple, but thick and sturdy, just like a well-used pale blue *kendogi*. Although undergoing many tribulations in the first half of his life, he nonetheless achieved great results as a kendoka after returning to his second home in Gunma, Japan. It seems that he did not talk about his experiences in Canada to those around. Few people, even kendo practitioners in Gunma, know of his history as a Canadian kendoka.

By contrast, Torao Mori was like an elegant silk cloth, soft and luxurious. He lived a fascinating life as though the sky was the limit, and all in the public eye. One can only assume that he was born under a lucky star. I am astonished by this man's good fortune as well as the brilliance of his life. It was no easy feat for a prewar Japanese to go to America for the first time and to be able to associate on equal footing with local Caucasians in such a short amount of time given the language barrier and differences in customs. Torao can be considered a man who attained the "American Dream", having relocated there after the war and achieved fame and financial success.

It is hoped that from reading these pages people can appreciate about how kendo took root and grew in Canada, in part due to the time and effort of these two men, and how that was then supported and continued by the passion and dedication of countless Japanese pioneers and following generations.

In Closing

I wrote this book to pay my respects to my senpai who demonstrated such a strong passion for kendo. I greatly appreciate their labours and other extraordinary figures in the kendo world. The continuation of kendo today would not have been possible without the hard work of the Nikkei pioneers discussed in this book.

Half a century has passed since Torao Mori's death and a quarter century since Motoo Matsushita passed away. Since then, the kendo environment has changed tremendously. The reality in North America is that kendo is gradually leaving the hands of the Nikkei. At the same time, the spread of kendo has been vast in Europe, where there is less history of Japanese immigration. It has been incredible to experience and witness these dynamic changes during my lifetime. When I close my eyes, I imagine small seeds being blown into fresh soil. These seeds will germinate and grow and end up producing wonderful fruit.

Lastly, my wish, then, is that "lifelong kendo" continues to take root across the world.

APPENDIX 1

Postwar Canadian Kendo Dojo/Clubs

Year Est.	Dojo Name	Founder(s) & Original Instructor(s)	Former & Current Instructor(s)	Major Events
1943	Raymond Kendo Club	Yuichi Akune	(closed: 1952)	
circa 1955	Steveston Kendo Club	Yuichi Akune Rintaro Hayashi Masao Hayashi	Moriharu Tanigami Ray Murao	
1964	Vancouver Kendo Club	Misaho Noda Eiji Omac Shigeru Kuwabara Kaoru Kimoto Masanobu Kawahira Takeharu Yoshimaru Hayaru Oyama	Yukio (Hirotaka) Ara Akira Hayashi Chozaburo Isa Makiko Hayashi (Ara) Takashi Yamada Natsuko Fukushima Akiko Fukushima	
	Toka Budokan	Masao L. Nakamura	(closed)	
1965	JCCC Kendo Club	Kaname Asa Morito Tsumura Koki Ariga Ron Ohnami	Morito Tsumura Koki Ariga Shigetaka Kamata Kiyoshi Hao Roy Asa Bryan Asa	
1966				Canadian Kendo Federation (CKF) founded.
1968	Manitoba Kendo Club	Ichiro Hirayama Risuke Hamade Tsune Amadatsu	Tsune Amadatsu N. Matsubara Tom Yamashita Taka Hattori Kyoko Miyata	
1970				1st World Kendo Championships in Tokyo, Japan.
1974	Calgary Kendo Club	Susumu Ikuta	Shuya Shiono (Advisor) Gerry Simon Blaine Campbell Dean Ara Stephen Moses Flora Chan	
	Immaculée-Conception Dojo de Kendo de Montreal	Douglas Funamoto Kiyoshi Ono	Douglas Funamoto Kiyoshi Ono (closed)	
1976	Montreal Kendo Club	Kiyoshi Ono	Junko Ariyama Martin Dore Julio Kenji Toida	
	Shidokan	Douglas Funamoto	Santoso Hanitijo Gilles Valiquette Yutaro Matsuura	
1977	Renbu Dojo	Hirotaka (Yukio) Ara	Hirotaka Ara Dean Ara	

Year Est.	Dojo Name	Founder(s) & Original Instructor(s)	Former & Current Instructor(s)	Major Events
	University of Toronto Kendo Club	Morito Tsumura David Johnson	David Johnson Toshi Hogi Matthew Raymond Tony Davidson	
1978	University of British Columbia Kendo Club	Hirokazu Okusa	Hirokazu Okusa David Harding Tsuyoshi Hamanaka	
	Hamilton Kendo Club	George Kumagai	George Kumagai Paul Morgan (closed:1996)	
	Ottawa Kendo Club	Mas Takahashi Makoto Inaba Masanori Arai Kensho Koshiji	Hughes Renaud Pierre Sasseville	
1980	University of Victoria Kendo Club	Ted Davis	Ted Davis Daisuke Hayashi	
	Laurentian Kendo Club	K.Tatsumi	Jeremie Charron Ben Mercer (closed)	
	Toronto Kendo Club (Fomerly Takubukan)	Shigeo Kimura	Shigeo Kimura Paul Nakamura Koichi Miyamoto Yuko Miyamoto	
	Etobicoke Kendo & Iaido Club	Shigetaka Kamata Koki Ariga	Shigetaka Kamata Kin Tak Ma Stephen Cruise Shigemitsu Kamata	
1981	Sunrise Kendo Club	Mitsuru Asaoka Takuo Uegaki	Mitsuru Asaoka Takuo Uegaki (closed)	
	Saskatoon Kendo Club	Ken Miyaoka	Ken Miyaoka Neil Gendzwill	
1984	Brantford / Renbukan Kendo & Iaido Club	Tamio Tateno	Tamio Tateno David Mori Geoff Carson (closed)	
	Kendo club de la Vieille Capitale	Gérard Blanchet Douglas Funamoto Gilles Valiquette	Douglas Funamoto Gilles Valiquette Claude Brisson	
	Quebec Kendo Kai	Hiroshi Awaga	Hiroshi Awaga Martin Doré	
1985	Marianapolis Kendo Club	Gabriel Weitzner	Gabriel Weitzner (closed)	
1986	Club de Kendo de l'Université de Montréal	Christian D'Orangeville Richard Goulet	Christian D'Orangeville Richard Goulet (closed: 2018)	
1987	Owen Sound Kendo Club	Jim Underwood Val Underwood	Jim Underwood Val Underwood	
	University of Waterloo Kendo Club	Shigetaka Kamata Taro Ariga	Shigetaka Kamata	
1989	St. Catharines Kendo Club	William Gill	William Gill (closed)	

Year Est.	Dojo Name	Founder(s) & Original Instructor(s)	Former & Current Instructor(s)	Major Events
1989	Tillsonburg Kendo Club	Paul Weaver	Paul Weaver Janet Weaver (closed)	
1990	McGill University Kendo Club	Christian D'Orangeville	Christian D'Orangeville	
circa 1990	University of Guelph Japanese wordsmanship Club (Sei Do Kai)	Goyo Ohmi (Iaido) Kim Taylor (Iaido, Jodo) Yasuhiro Mori (Kendo)	Kim Taylor (Iaido,Jodo) (kendo closed)	
1991				8th World Kendo Championships held in Toronto, Canada.
	Club de Kendo Isshin	Gilles Valiquette	Gilles Valiquette	
1996	Century Kumdo Club (formerly Central Kumdo Club until 2017)	Junho Lee	Junho Lee	
	Matsukai Kendo & Iaido Club	Bruce Campbell	Bruce Campbell	
	Burlington Kendo Club	Paul Morgan Tsuneo Yamazaki Andreas Drasener	Paul Morgan Michael Robertson Ed Yamashita	
	Mississauga Kendo Club	Shigeo Kimura Richard Tizzard Glenn Yamada	Shigeo Kimura Glenn Yamada	
1997	York University Kendo Club	Sung Hwan Kim	Kiyoshi Hao	
	Regina Kendo Club	Ken Miyaoka Hiroaki Izumi	Kouichi Tada Mike Wagner Yusuke Yanai	
1998	Youshinkan Dojo Canada	Mitsuru Asaoka	Mitsuru Asaoka Motoki Asaoka Suguru Asaoka	
	IKSDK(Il Kum Soon Do Kwan)	Soon Do Park	Soon Do Park Minwoo Park	
	Tateyama Kendo & Iaido Club	Michael Attard Frank Blander David Green	Michael Attard David Badour Chris Jarvie	
1999	Dalhousie Kendo Club / Halifax Kendo Club	Mark MacLeod Yoko Nonaka	Steve Quinlan Sung Lee (closed)	
	Cambridge Kendo Club	Toshi Hogi	Toshi Hogi	
2000	Edmonton Kendo Club	Stephanie Bozzor	Stephanie Bozzor Stephen Hladky	
	Simon Fraser University Kendo Club	Hirokazu Okusa	Hirokazu Okusa David Chiu	
	Forest City Kendo Club	David Mori	David Mori Shigehide Miyagawa Hidekazu Nishigori	
	Isshin Saint-Jean	Jean-Pierre Angers Gilles Valiquette	Jean-Pierre Angers (closed)	
2001	Kelowna Kendo Club	Victor Nishi Steve Choi Greg Reschke	Victor Nishi Greg Reschke	

Year Est.	Dojo Name	Founder(s) & Original Instructor(s)	Former & Current Instructor(s)	Major Events
	Jung Ko Kendo	Jin Whan Lee	Morito Tsumura Jin Whan Lee Hyun June Choi	
	University of Western Ontario Kendo Club	David Mori	David Mori Shigehide Miyagawa Hidekazu Nishigori Thopik Adianto	
2002	Higashikaze Iaido & Kendo Club	Bill Anderson Dave Green	Bill Anderson (Iaido) Loic D'Orangeville (Kendo)	
2004	The Rock Kendo Club	Rodolphe Devillers	Sean Ryan Wilson Humphries	
	Niagara Kendo Club (formerly Hayakawa Kendo Club)	Mark Kawabe	Mark Kawabe	
	Club de Kendo Granby	Michel Duquette Richard Goulet	Michel Duquette	
2005	Milton Kendo Club	Paul Morgan	Paul Morgan	
	Club de Kendo AMS (Académie Martiale Serei)	Richard Goulet	Richard Goulet François St-Germain (closed: 2017)	
2006	Kingston Kendo Club	Stephen Quinlan	Stephen Quinlan	
	Nikka Gakuen Kendo Club	Parents of Nikka Gakuen School Akihito Hamaba Hideki Sumi	Akihito Hamaba Hideki Sumi (closed)	
2008	Algoma Kendo Club	Brian Lampe Hyun June Choi	Brian Lampe Hyun June Choi Matt Keenan Jennifer Brown	
	Ryerson University Kendo Club	Shigeo Kimura Eric CharlesChiu	Shigeo Kimura Eric CharlesChiu	
2009	Winnipeg Kendo Club	Corie Namba	Corie Namba	
2010	Tozenji Kendo Club	Toshihiro Hamanaka	Toshihiro Hamanaka Tsuyoshi Hamanaka Miyako Oka	
	Markham Kendo Club	Hideki Sumi	Morito Tsumura Hideki Sumi	
2011	Chinook Kendo Dojo	Kyle Lee JeongRyul Lee	Kyle Lee Daisaku Taguchi	
				CKF Centenary celebration held in Vancouver.
2012	Carleton University Kendo Club	Sujan Park	Sujan Park Masanori Arai Daniel Lau	
2013	Hamilton Kendo Club (revisited)	Shigeo Kimura Yukio Yamada	Yukio Yamada Richard Tizzard	
2015	Tesshin Dojo	David Westhead	David Westhead	
	Stratford Kendo Club	David Mori Shigehide Miyagawa Derek Barr	David Mori Shigehide Miyagawa Derek Barr	
2016	Dojo de Kendo Saint-Jean	Jean-Pierre Angers	Jean-Pierre Angers	

Year Est.	Dojo Name	Founder(s) & Original Instructor(s)	Former & Current Instructor(s)	Major Events
2017	Lethbridge Kendo Club	Ryun Kim Kyle Lee	Kyle Lee Ryun Kim	
	Halifax ShuuRenKan	Steve Harris Jay Howard Ryota Suyama	Ryota Suyama Steve Harris Michael Robertson	
	Newmarket Kendo Club	Toshi Hogi Michelle de Bourbon	Toshi Hogi	
	Kitajima Kendo	Frédéric Mayer Juan Schneider	Juan Schneider	
2018	Whitewater Kendo Club	Michael Underwood Hideki Sumi	Michael Underwood	
2019	Barrhaven Kendo Club	John Maisonneuve	John Maisonneuve	
	Club de Kendō Ayame	Richard Goulet	Richard Goulet	
	KIPPON Dojo	Antoine Fortier	Antoine Fortier	

Canadian Kendo Club Establishments and Connections to 2000

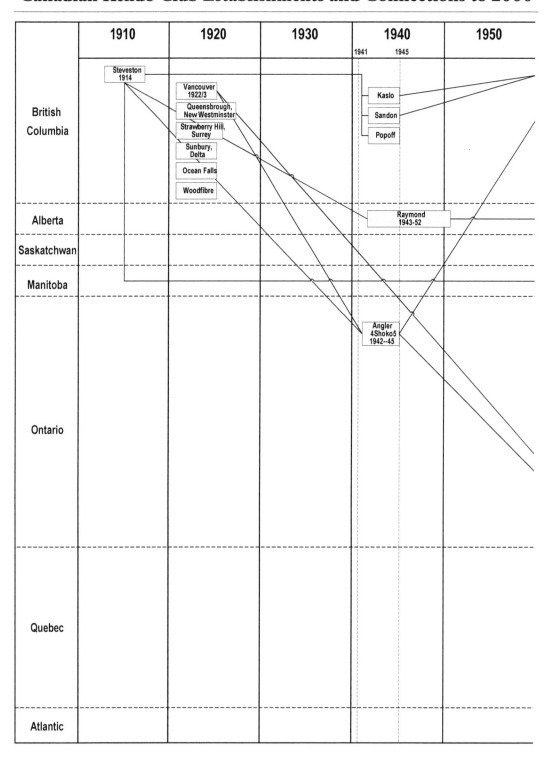

	1910	1920	1930	1940	1950

British Columbia

Steveston 1914
Vancouver 1922/3
Queensbrough, New Westminster
Strawberry Hill, Surrey
Sunbury, Delta
Ocean Falls
Woodfibre
Kaslo
Sandon
Popoff

Alberta

Raymond 1943-52

Saskatchwan

Manitoba

Angler 4Shoko5 1942--45

Ontario

Quebec

Atlantic

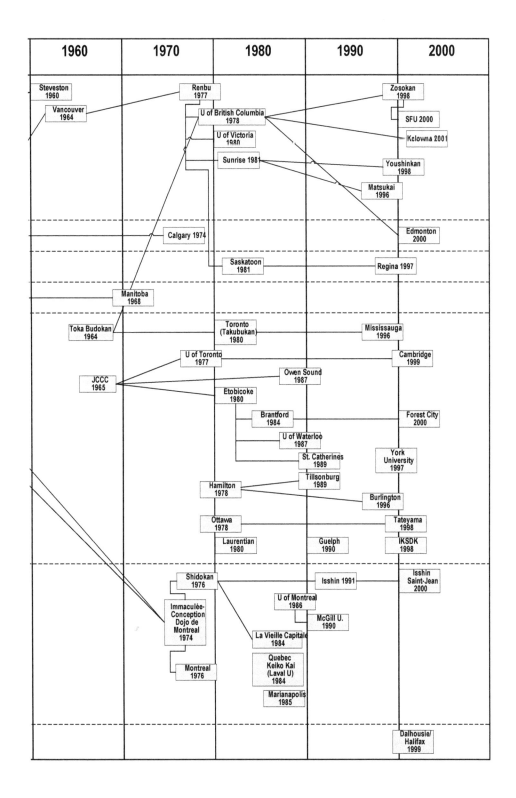

	1960	1970	1980	1990	2000

Steveston 1960
Vancouver 1964
Renbu 1977
U of British Columbia 1978
U of Victoria 1980
Sunrise 1981
Zosokan 1998
SFU 2000
Kelowna 2001
Youshinkan 1998
Matsukai 1996

Calgary 1974
Edmonton 2000

Saskatoon 1981
Regina 1997

Manitoba 1968

Toka Budokan 1964
Toronto (Takubukan) 1980
Mississauga 1996

U of Toronto 1977
Cambridge 1999

JCCC 1965
Owen Sound 1987
Etobicoke 1980
Brantford 1984
Forest City 2000
U of Waterloo 1987
St. Catherines 1989
York University 1997
Tillsonburg 1989
Hamilton 1978
Burlington 1996
Ottawa 1978
Tateyama 1998
Laurentian 1980
Guelph 1990
IKSDK 1998

Shidokan 1976
Isshin 1991
Isshin Saint-Jean 2000
Immaculée-Conception Dojo de Montreal 1974
U of Montreal 1986
McGill U. 1990
La Vieille Capitale 1984
Montreal 1976
Quebec Keiko Kai (Laval U) 1984
Marianapolis 1985
Dalhousie/ Halifax 1999

91

APPENDIX 3

World Kendo Championships
—Team Canada Delegation Members and Results—

Year / Host Country	Delegation Head	Manager	Coach	Officer(s)	Competitors		Individual Awards	Team Awards
1WKC 1970 Japan			Misaho Noda		Yukio Ara Jim Murray Gordon Gartly	Hiromi Hori Kazuko Nakamura Ichiya Mochizuki		
2WKC 1973 USA	Misaho Noda	Rintaro Hayashi, Masao Hayashi	Moriharu Tanigami	Jim Murray	Morito Tsumura Koki Ariga M. Ogawa Yukio Ara Shigetaka Kamata Gordon Gartly Kiyosh Hao	Kuni Ikuta Alan Takasaki Tak Yoshida Roy Asa Ichiya Mochizuki W. Williams	Fighting Sprit Award: Kiyoshi Hao	Men's Team 2nd Place
3WKC 1976 England	Misaho Noda	William Anderson	Morito Tsumura	R. Johnson	Morito Tsumura Koki Ariga Kiyoshi Hao Shigetaka Kamata Roy Asa Yuji. Ohara	Sanji Kanno Tak Yoshida Alan Takasaki Walter Iwata Ray Murao	Fighting Sprit Award: Roy Asa	Men's Team 2nd Place
4WKC 1979 Japan	Misaho Noda	Ron Onami	Morito Tsumura	K. Ono, Jim Murray	Koki Ariga Kiyoshi Hao Shigetaka Kamata Ray Murao Roy Asa Alvin Noda	David Johnson Alan Takasaki Dwight Noda Brian Takama Allan Hill Anthony Morimoto	Fighting Sprit Award: Ray Murao	
5WKC 1982 Brazil	Roy Asa	Morito Tsumura	Koki Ariga, Tsumura Kosaku (advisor)	Ron Ohnami (Asst Mgr)	Morito Tsumura Koki Ariga Kiyoshi Hao Shigetaka Kamata Shigeo Kimura Ray Murao	Mike Shizuru David Johnson Dwight Noda Mark Noda Pat Okano Paul Ohnami	Fighting Sprit Award: Shigetaka Kamata	
6WKC 1985 France	Roy Asa	Morito Tsumura	Kiyoshi Hao	Shuzo Uyenaka, Ron Ohnami	Shigetaka Kamata Shigeo Kimura Ray Murao Dwight Noda Mark Noda David Johnson	David Brownell Bryan Asa Paul Ohnami Robert Noguchi Glen Harada Terry Kondo	Fighting Sprit Award: David Johnson	Men's Team 3rd Place

Year / Host Country	Delegation Head	Manager	Coach	Officer(s)	Competitors		Individual Awards	Team Awards
7WKC 1988 Korea	Roy Asa	Morito Tsumura	Kiyoshi Hao	Ken Oda, Kiyoshi Ono, Ron Ohnami, Shuzo Uyenaka, Sanji Kanno	Shane Kamata Shigeo Kimura Ray Murao David Johnson Mark Noda Glenn Harada	Bryan Asa Paul Ohnami Terry Kondo Taro Ariga Philip Nishikihama Jason Ohnami		Men's Team 3rd Place Fighting Sprit Award: Ray Murao
8WKC 1991 Canada	Roy Asa	Shigeo Kimura	Shane Kamata	Ron Ohnami, Shuzo Uyenaka	Christian D'Orangeville Ray Murao Mark Noda Tony Davidson Steve Nakatsu Bryan Asa Alex Shirran	Taro Ariga Terry Kondo Shane Asa Philip Nishikihama Eric Ohara Motoki Asaoka		Men's Team 3rd Place Fighting Sprit Award: Ray Murao
9WKC 1994 France	Roy Asa	Shigeo Kimura	Ray Murao	K. Hao (assistant), C. D'Orangeville (assistant)	Mark Noda Glenn Harada Tony Davidson Steve Nakatsu Bryan Asa Alex Shirran	Taro Ariga David Mori Philip. Nishikihama Matthew Raymond Motoki Asaoka Suguru Asaoka		Men's Team 3rd Place
10WKC 1997 Japan	Roy Asa	Morito Tsumura	Ray Murao		Mark Noda Glenn Harada Tony Davidson Bryan Asa Taro Ariga	Terry Kondo Philip Nishikihama Matthew Raymond Motoki Asaoka Suguru Asaoka		Fighting Sprit Award: Philip Nishikihama
					Chiharu Hao Corie Namba Mireille Palaysi Yuki Hayashi Susan Choi Wendy Nakano	Maya Taguchi Makiko Hayashi Yuriko Sugiyama Nancy Yeung Stephanie Harding	(3-dan and Up) Wendy Nakano 3rd Place Fighting Sprit Award: Chiharu Hao	
11WKC 2000 USA	Roy Asa	Richard Tizzard	Ray Murao		Taro Ariga Bryan Asa Philip Nishikihama Motoki Asaoka Matthew Raymond	Dean Ara Suguru Asaoka Daisaku Taguchi Eddie Yamashita Shigemitsu Kamata	Fighting Sprit Award: Suguru Asaoka Dean Ara	Men's Team 3rd Place
			Mark Noda		Wendy Nakano Makiko Hayashi Maya Taguchi Hana Ariga	Misato Akitaya Chiharu Hao Corie Namba	Fighting Sprit Award: Wendy Nakano	Women's Team 3rd Place

Year / Host Country	Delegation Head	Manager	Coach	Officer(s)	Competitors		Individual Awards	Team Awards
12WKC 2003 Scotland	Roy Asa	Richard Tizzard	Ray Murao		Taro Ariga Suguru Asaoka Matthew Raymond Daisaku Taguchi Dean Ara	Eddy Yamashita Shigemitsu Kamata Kiyotaka Kamata Takashi Yamada	Fighting Sprit Award: Suguru Asaoka	Fighting Sprit Award: Daisaku Taguchi
			Mark Noda		Wendy Robillard Takako Matisz Misato Akitaya Hana Ariga	Chiharu Hao Natsuko Fukushima Makiko Hayashi		Women's Team 3rd Place
13WKC 2006 Taiwan	Roy Asa	Richard Tizzard, Bryan Asa	Ray Murao		Dean Ara Taro Ariga Matthew Raymond Suguru Asaoka	Daisaku Taguchi Robin Tanaka Ben Shirahama Shigemitsu Kamata	Fighting Sprit Award: Shigemitsu Kamata	Fighting Sprit Award: Daisaku Taguchi
			Wendy Robillard		Makiko Hayashi Maya Taguchi Yuki Hayashi Chiharu Hao	Natsuko Fukushima Shiho Kamata Akiko Fukushima Wendy Robillard	Fighting Sprit Award: Makiko Hayashi	Women's Team 3rd Place
14WKC 2009 Brazil	Roy Asa	David Johnson	Bryan Asa		Daisaku Taguchi Suguru Asaoka Shigemitsu Kamata Eddie Yamashita	Takashi Yamada Hyun-June Choi Antoine Fortier Kyle Eunseob Lee		Fighting Sprit Award: Shigemitsu Kamata
			Dean Ara		Maya Taguchi Natsuko Fukushima Akiko Fukushima Yumiko Hayashi	Keiko Marumo Man San Ma Hanaca Yamada Misato Hamanaka	Fighting Sprit Award: Misato Hamanaka	Fighting Sprit Award: Natsuko Fukushima
15WKC 2012 Italy	Hirokazu Okusa	David Mori	Matthew Raymond		Suguru Asaoka Shigemitsu Kamata Eddie Yamashita Takashi Yamada Ryo Tamaru	Tuan-Anh Hoang Elliott Alitilia Tsuyoshi Hamanaka (Dev Prospect)	Fighting Sprit Award: Tuan-Anh Hoang	
			Daisuke Hayashi		Maya Taguchi Akiko Fukushima Tania Delage Bree Yang Man-San Ma	Hanaca Yamada Misato Hamanaka Ayaka Sugiyama (Dev Prospect)		

Year / Host Country	Delegation Head	Manager	Coach	Officer(s)	Competitors		Individual Awards	Team Awards
16WKC 2015 Japan	Christian D'Orangeville	Ray Murao	Matthew Raymond	Manabu Ogawa (Trainer)	Shigemitsu Kamata Ryo Tamaru Edgar Yamashita Takashi Yamada Kyle Lee	Tuan Anh Hoang Elliott Altilia Tsuyoshi Hamanaka Eiji Kita		
			Daisuke Hayashi		Akiko Fukushima Hanaca Yamada ManSan Ma Juneko Kurahashi	Ayaka Sugiyama Bree Yang Bora Choi Kyrene Kim	Fighting Sprit Award: Hanaca Yamada	Fighting Sprit Award: Bree Yang
17WKC 2018 Korea	Christian D'Orangeville	Ray Murao	Dean Ara	Manabu Ogawa (Trainer)	Eun Seob Lee Ryo Yasumura Elliott Altilia Hyoung Joon Kim	Kunhee Kim Eiji Kita Edgar Yamashita		
			Dean Ara, Edgar Yamashita (Assistant Coach)		Hanaca Yamada Akiko Fukushima Man-San Ma Bree Yang	Kyrene Kim Sunmin Kim Kianna Darbyshire Francesca Ho		Women's Team 3rd Place
Based on WKC Programs with some amendments								

APPENDIX 4

Postwar Canadian Kendo Federation Officers

Years	President	Treasurer	Secretary	Major events
1966–1969?	Yuichi Akune		Yoshikazu Kimura	Formation of federation between BC and Ontario.
1969?–1980	Misao Noda			- Many exchanges with Japan. - Beginning of participation in World Kendo Championships.
1980–2009	Roy T. Asa	Peter Dunning Sanji Kanno Cathy Lenius Gary Nakajima (from 1988)	Shuzo Uenaka Kiyoshi Hao Stephen Cruise (from1988)	- Nationwide organization of Canadian kendo begins. - 8th World Kendo Championship held in Toronto, Canada.
2009–2014	Hirokazu Okusa	John Maisonneuve	Kim Taylor, Tadashi.Wakabayashi Neil Gendzwill	- Celebrated 100th Anniversary of Kendo in Canada. - New By-law of C.K.F and various regulations created and revised.
2014 to present (as of 2019)	Christian D'Orangeville	John Maisonneuve	Neil Gendzwill	

APPENDIX 5

Life Events of Motoo Matsushita and Torao Mori

Year	Motoo Matsushita (1918–1991)	Torao Mori (1914–1969) * from the book *The Man Called Tiger Mori*	Major Global Events and Related Matters
1914		Born to Yasu and Zenjiro Mori as their fourth son. He had three older brothers and five sisters.	
1918	Born in British Columbia, Canada.		
1922		Adopted by Seiji Noma at age eight.	
1924?	Returns to Japan to receive education at around age six.		
	Learns kendo around grade 5 at Maebashi City Jonan Elementary School.		
	Takes part as a Gunma representative in Meiji Shrine Athletic Meet at elementary Grade six, and finishes runner up.		
	After graduating from primary school, enters Gunma Prefectural Maebashi Commercial High School and joins its kendo club.		
1925			Noma Dojo completed/opened.
1929		Adopted. Surname changed from Noma to Mori.	Worldwide recession. Tokichi Nakamura goes to US.
1930			Seiji Mochida invited as head instructor at Noma Dojo.
1931			Waseda University Kendo Club goes on its first overseas tour led by Sazaburo Takano.
1932		Graduates from Sugamo Middle School, employed by daily o*Hochi Shinbun*.	Manchurian crisis, Manchu-koku.
1934		Defeated by Hisashi Noma in the Tokyo heat finals of the *tenranjiai*.	
1935		Recruited by the armed forces and sent to China	
1936	Returns to Canada at age 19. Serves as instructor at Isshinkai Kendo Club in Woodfibre, BC. Later becomes head instructor with Yoshinkan Kendo Club in Vancouver, teaching some 60 Japanese Canadians.		

Year	Motoo Matsushita (1918–1991)	Torao Mori (1914–1969) * from the book *The Man Called Tiger Mori*	Major Global Events and Related Matters
1937		Travels to Los Angeles, USA under directive of Dai-Nippon Butoku Kai (Greater Japan Martial Virtue Society). Arrives in Honolulu on January 28. Arrives in LA on March 19. Takes up fencing at University of Southern California.	Tokichi Nakamura returns from US. Waseda University Kendo Club goes on its second tour of LA led by Sasaburo Takano. The team makes a stop in Vancouver to give kendo instruction.
1938		Champion at the California State Fencing Championship. Takes part as Western Region representative in US Fencing Championship in April, losing in the finals. Returns to Japan in July and joins the Imperial Army. Sent to Manchuria to join a tank corp. In October, Seiji Noma and Hisashi Noma pass away in quick succession.	
1940		Married to Janice Teiko Akaboshi, a Japanese American nisei, in Japan. Janice stays on in Japan until the war's end.	Tokyo Olympic Games cancelled.
1941	At age 23, the Pacific War breaks out.		Pearl Harbor attacked.
1942	Forced relocation of Nikkei people begins. Sent to the Angler POW Camp.	Has a *shiai* against his sensei Seiji Mochida in a Japan-Manchuria competition.	
1943	Kendo club Shoko Dojo is formed at the Angler camp on August 22. Starts teaching as head instructor.		
1944	Shoko Dojo holds first anniversary commemoration competition.		Noma Dojo is closed.
1945	Shoko Dojo holds second anniversary commemoration competition. Camp is closed as war ends. Relocates to Moose Jaw.	As air raids on Tokyo intensify, evacuates to Kiryu.	War ends, kendo is prohibited.
1946	Sent back to Japan at age 28.		
1950		Returns to the US.	
1951		Joins the Southern California Kendo Dan Holders' Association.	
1953			Kendo ban is lifted and All Japan Kendo Federation inaugurated.
1955	Takes part in 3rd Japan Prefectural/Municipal Competition. (Takes part in the same annual competition for 7 years in succession.) Thereafter wins 6-dan and 7-dan category of the 5th Nikko Kendo Competition.	US Kendo Federation inaugurated. Appointed the first President of the US Kendo Federation. Receives 8th dan from the Federation. Arranges US tour by five members of Meiji University Kendo Club.	Hawaii Kendo Federation inaugurated.
1956		Goes on study tour of Japan with disciples, observes 4th All Japan Kendo Championship.	

Year	Motoo Matsushita (1918–1991)	Torao Mori (1914–1969) * from the book *The Man Called Tiger Mori*	Major Global Events and Related Matters
1957		Arranges Japan-US Kendo Goodwill Exchange All-star competition. Visit by Japanese student all-star teams.	
1958	Takes part in 5th Japan East-West Kendo Competition.		
1959	Takes part in the 7th All Japan Kendo Championship at age 41. (Thereafter takes part in the same championship three years in a row.)		Brazil Kendo Federation inaugurated.
1960		Takes part in Rome Olympic Games as coach of US fencing team.	
1961	Receives 7-dan at age 43.		
1962			Junzo Sasamori goes to Sao Paulo to give kendo instruction.
1963		Arranges for Yūji Oasa, Takashi Ozawa, Shinsuke Masuda, Toshio Watanabe and Kazuto Toshioka to visit the US and Sao Paulo, Brazil, to give kendo instruction. Torao sets up Mori Securities.	
1964		Takes part in Tokyo Olympic Games as US fencing team coach.	
1965			Canadian Kendo Federation inaugurated. Hiromasa Takano gives kendo instruction in Canada.
1966		Gives kendo instruction in Vancouver and Toronto.	
1967	Visits Vancouver, thereafter touring Toronto, LA and elsewhere to observe Kendo activities.	Closes down Mori Securities, sets up Mori Fencing Academy.	1st International Goodwill Kendo Competition held.
1968		Takes part in Mexico City Olympic Games as US fencing team coach.	
1969		Passes away during a kendo practice from a heart attack on January 8, age 54.	
1970			1st World Kendo Championship is held.
1991	Passes away at age 73.		
***	Other than competitions mentioned above, takes part in National Athletic Competition four times as Gunma Prefecture representative.		

APPENDIX 6

Rod Nobuto Omoto (1918-2013)

I would like to introduce another notable kendoka who should be remembered as someone who was active on both sides of the Pacific at the same time as Motoo and Torao. Nobuto (Rod) Omoto was a Hawaii-born Nisei, who went to Japan at age 20 to enroll in the Budo Senmon Gakko (Busen), a school for training young men and women in martial arts. He was born the same year as Motoo and was four years younger than Torao Mori.

He trained more or less as a live-in disciple under Kin'nosuke Ogawa. As Busen was disbanded due to the war, he trained there for only two years. Nevertheless, he received a diploma as one of its last graduates. He risked death several times with the Japanese Imperial Army and witnessed the hell of the atomic bomb attack on Hiroshima.

After the war, Nobuto worked as an interpreter for GHQ (General Headquarters), the allied occupation forces in Japan after World War II. He ended up remaining in Japan for 26 years. In 1960, he returned to America and settled in Tacoma, near Seattle. He used to give lectures on the 17th century master Musashi Miyamaoto's *Gorin no sho* (The Book of Five Rings) at a local college. Nobuto mentioned that he met Torao on several occasions at tournaments in Hawaii and on the west coast of the US and Canada.

Rod Nobuto Omoto, one of the last *Busen* graduates.

Excerpts From the Booklet *Kanada no kendo ryakushi* (Kendo in Canada to 1946)

Published by the Canadian Kendo Federation in 2011

Description of the Documents

By Tadashi Wakabayashi

[1] 林林太郎「加奈太剣道略史」: *Kanada no Kendo Ryakushi* (**An Outline of Kendo in Canada**) by Hayashi Rintaro is dated 11 March 1967. He composed it at the request of Matsushita Moto, but did not publish it. Instead, the manuscript was held in trust by Shigeru Kuwabara until January 2011. This valuable document is the *starting point* for writing a history of kendo in Canada. Hayashi did not cite references in this sketchy "Outline History," so we must assume that he simply jotted down events from memory in 1967, and did not base himself on records. As a result, there are some clear errors in his work, such as identifying Takano Hiromasa as a lecturer in kendo at the University of California. Also, we have no idea what events and persons, or how many of these events and persons, he omitted from his account whether on purpose or more likely, unwittingly. In response to a private request by Morito Tsumura, Hayashi wrote a letter on 13 April 1980 that also describes the history of kendo in Canada in a bit more detail with a few pieces of new information. For example, he mentions an exhibition of *gekken* [撃剣] or "attacking with swords"—an earlier form of kendo—during a celebratory event in Steveston in 1889 to mark the marriage of the crown prince and later Taisho emperor. Yet this 1980 letter contradicts Hayashi's "Outline History" on a few points as well, for example, the year in which Steveston Yokikan was founded, whether 1913 or 1914. My English translation below covers the portion of his "Outline History" down to 1945, the end of World War II. Given the lack of alternatives, we are forced to rely on Hayashi, especially for the pre-1941 period. It is hoped that other sources will supplement his meager content and verify or gainsay his accuracy.

[2] 「明け行く松湖」: *Akeyuku Shoko* (**The Dawning of Pine Lake**) is a collection of records left by kendo club members at Angler Interment Camp. Two hand-produced copies now exist. Its editorial board consisted of Ichikawa Haruo 1st-Dan, Hibi Katashi 2nd-Dan, and Furukawa Sakuzoo 1st-Dan. The Angler prison camp housed German and Italian POWs captured

earlier in the war, which for Canada began in September 1939. It accepted Japanese and Japanese-Canadian inmates starting in July 1942. As a POW camp under armed military guard and encircled by three layers of barbed wire, Angler differed decisively from the relatively free and open "relocation camps" like Slocan or Kaslo that were intended as a temporary first stop in their inhabitants' eventual dispersal east of the Rockies. In those relocation camps, for example, Japanese and Japanese-Canadians did not have to wear prison uniforms and were not subject to military-style roll call and work details at set times every day as was true at Angler. Rightly or wrongly, the BC provincial and Canadian federal governments deemed that the men sent to Angler (which housed no women or males under 18) were disloyal enemy aliens who posed a danger to national security.

In an interview on 18 May 2011, Hibi stated that Ichikawa authored most of the unsigned pieces in the work including *Shoko dojo haten-ki* [松湖道場發展記 , The Development of Pine Lake Dojo]. Ichikawa, Hibi, and Furukawa began compiling the book in August 1944 and completed it in April 1945. It was hand-copied mainly by Hibi with help from a language teacher named "Miyazaki sensei" who may have been the former principal of Fairview Japanese School in the Vancouver-Burnaby area. In his 13 April 1980 letter to Morito Tsumura, Hayashi Rintaro mentioned that kendo practices took place at this school in the prewar period.

"The Development of Pine Lake Dojo" exudes zealous Japanese nationalism and militarism—garnished with emperor worship and support for Yasukuni Shrine—that may not reflect the views held by most dojo members. This loyalty to Japan's cause was more popular among Japanese-Canadians than we usually assume today. David Suzuki wrote that, at Slocan, "My peers sometimes echoed their parents' bitterness and hoped Japan would kick the hell out of the Allies…. As a result, I was often beaten up at school." Nakano Takeo, a fellow Angler prisoner who did not practice kendo, said that chauvinists, called "*ganbariya*" back then, "numbered in the hundreds at Angler and their views won the ascendancy." Overall, however, the documents I translate do not support Nakano's assertion. Equally important, the motivation behind pro-Japan sentiment is unclear. Did these men desire a Japanese victory to start with? Or did they become that way owing to racial prejudice in Canadian society, the robbery of their assets by BC neighbors, and unjust imprisonment by the Canadian government? Or was a combination of factors at work? These questions require further research before conclusions can be drawn.

Many Angler inmates, including dojo members, had joined the Nisei Mass Evacuation Group mentioned by Hori Tatsuo, Kawahira Masanobu, and Ueyama Masakazu. This group engaged in a highly principled, albeit violent, defiance of federal government orders to join work camps and to remove men beyond a "protected area" 100 miles from the BC coastline. They held that such orders broke up families in contrast to the US government's method of relocating Japanese-American families intact at that time. After German and Italian POWs were removed from Angler, its population of Japanese and Japanese-Canadian prisoners stood at 767 in 1942 and fell to about 430 when Angler closed in April 1946, eight and a half months after the war ended in August 1945.

BIBLIOGRAPHY

Arai Shunichi (ed.): *Suen Kenyu No.10: Mori Torao Tsuito-go*, Sugamo Gakuen Kenyu-kai, Tokyo: 1969.

Hayase Toshiyuki: *Taiga Mori to yobareta otoko* (The Man They Called Tiger Mori), Ski Journal Publisher Inc., Tokyo: 1991.

Hanazono Mitsunori: *Kendo no fukkatsu* (The Revival of Kendo), Kodansha, Tokyo: 1978.

Kobayashi, Luis: *Burajiru kendo no rekishi – chosa to gaiyo* (History of Kendo in Brazil - Survey and Outline), Sao Paulo Institute of Human Sciences, Sao Paulo: 2008.

Angler P.O.W. Camp Shoko Dojo Members: *Akeyuku shoko* (The Dawning of Pine Lake), private publication – handwritten: 1945.

Okazaki, Robert K.: *The Nisei Mass Evacuation Group and P.O.W. '101'*, Angler, Ontario, self–published: 1996.

Okazaki, Robert K: *Angura, Ontario Senji horyo shuyojo #101* (Angler, Ontario P.O.W Camp #101), self-published: 1992.

Hayashi Rintaro: *Kuroshio no hate ni* (Beyond the Japanese Current), Japan Publications Inc, Tokyo: 1974.

Hayashi Rintaro: *Kouhan mandan* (Banter on the Riverside), self-published: 1988.

Hayashi Rintaro: *Kanada no kendo ryakuji* (An Outline of Kendo in Canada), unpublished: 1967.

Niiho Mitsuru: *Ishi wo mote oarurugotoku* (Chased Away with a Stone), Japan Publications Inc., Tokyo: 1975.

Canadian Kendo Federation: *Kendo in Canada to 1946*: 2011

Gunma Kendo Renmei: *Gunma kendo renmei kendo shi* (Gunma Kendo Federation's History of

Kendo), Gunma Kendo Federation: 1998.

All Japan Kendo Federation: *Zen nihon kendo renmei senshuken kiroku* (Records of All Japan Kendo Federation Championships).

Omoto, Rod and Omoto, Charlotte: *Autobiography of Rod Omoto*, self-published: 2015.

Nichols, Doug: *"Mori and Kendo"*, West Coast Fencing Archive: July 8, 2019. (https://www. westcoastfencingarchive.com/2019/07/08/mori-and-kendo/ - Accessed November 9, 2020)

Yamaga Yasutaro (Hashizume W.T. trans.): *History of Haney Nokai (Farmer's Association)*, 4 Print Division of Musson Copy Centres Inc., North York, Ontario: 2006.

Letters

Motoo Matsushita (while interned in Angler) to Rintaro Hayashi: November 20, 1945.

Rintaro Hayashi to Ichiro Hirayama (residing in Winnipeg, Manitoba): February 22, 1966.

Rintaro Hayashi to Morito Tsumura (residing in Toronto, Ontario): April 13, 1980.

Ron Akune to author: February 20, 2020.

Photo and Map Credits

Library and Archives Canada – LAC
Nikkei National Museum – NNM
University of British Columbia Archives – UBC

Chapter 1

Figure 1-1: Map by John Endo Greenaway
1-1: NNM 1994.81.9
1-2: LAC MIKAN 4052085
1-3: UBC Archives JCPC.25.117
1-4: LAC MIKAN 4052096
1-5: LAC MIKAN 4052081
1-6: LAC MIKAN 4052072
1-7: LAC MIKAN 4052075
1-8: NNM 1994.82.10.1
Figure 1-2: Map by John Endo Greenaway
Figure 1-3: NNM 1994.69.1
1-9: NNM 1996.178.1.15
1-10: NNM 2011.19.15
1-11: NNM 1994.86.2
1-12: Rintaro Hayashi private collection
1-13: NNM 2010.23.2.4.514
1-14: Rintaro Hayashi private collection
1-15: NNM 2001.9.062
1-16: NNM 2001.9.065

Chapter 2

2-1: NNM 2010.80.2.72
2-2: History of Haney Nokai, p.91
Figure 2-1: Historical Atlas of Vancouver, Douglas & McIntyre Ltd, 2007, p.67
2-3: CVA 260-106
2-4: Rintaro Hayashi Private Collection

2-5: Rintaro Hayashi private collection
2-6: Rintaro Hayashi private collection
2-7: NNM 2012.40.2.003
2-8: NNM 2010.35.2-2.001
2-9: Rintaro Hayashi Private Collection
2-10: NNM 2010.35.2.2.12
2-11: NNM 2010.35.2.2.003
2-12: NNM 2010.35.2.2.11
2-13: Rintaro Hayashi private collection
2-14: NNM 2012.40.2.5
2-15: NNM 2012.40.2.006

Chapter 3

3-1: NNM 2010.23.2.4.517
3-2: LAC MIKAN
3-3: LAC MIKAN
3-4: NNM 2010.35.2.2.31
3-5: NNM 2010-35-2-2-021
3-6: NNM 2010.35.2.2.5
3-7: Mark Noda private collection
3-8: Rintaro Hayashi private collection
3-9: Rintaro Hayashi private collection
3-10: Glen Yamada collection
3-11: Hirokazu Okusa private collection
3-12: NNM 2010.35.2.249
3-13: Unknown source
3-14: NNM 2012.40.2.026
3-15: Akira Hayashi Private Collection
3-16: Hirokazu Okusa private collection
3-17: Makiko Ara collection
3-18: Hirokazu Okusa private collection
3-19: Hirokazu Okusa private collection
3-20: Courtesy Neil Gendzwill
3-21: NNM 2012.40.2.35
3-22: Canadian Kendo Federation

Chapter 4

4-1: Rintaro Hayashi private collection

4-2: Courtesy Kendo Nihon Ltd, Japan

4-3: Rintaro Hayashi private collection

4-4: Unknown

4-5: NNM 2011.68.1.71

4-6: Mark Noda private collection

4-7: Hirokazu Okusa private collection

4-8: From the book *The Man They Called Tiger Mori*

4-9: Courtesy Kendo Nihon Ltd, Japan

4-10: Courtesy Kendo Nihon Ltd, Japan

4-11: Pat Murosako private collection

4-12: Pat Murosako private collection

4-13: Pat Murasako private collection

4-14: Courtesy Luis Kobayashi, Brazil

4-15: Courtesy Luis Kobayashi, Brazil

4-16: Courtesy Kendo Nihon Ltd, Japan

4-17: Courtesy Kendo Nihon Ltd, Japan

4-18: NNM 2012.40.2.16

4-19: Hirokazu Okusa private collection

4-20: NNM 2010.35.2.1.57

4-21: NNM 2010.35.2.28

4-22: NNM 2010.35.2.24

4-23: NNM 2010.35.2.30

4-24: NNM 2012.40.2.8

GLOSSARY

Japanese Canadian Terminology

Nikkei	日系	People of Japanese ancestry living outside of Japan.
Issei	一世	First generation to immigrate to Canada.
Nisei	二世	Second generation, the first born in Canada.
Kika-Nisei	帰化一世	Second generation, sent to Japan but returned to Canada.
Sansei	三世	Third generation.

Kendo Terminology*

bogu	防具	Equipment used in kendo. (Also *kendo-gu*.)
bokuto	木刀	A wooden sword
do	胴	The piece of kendo equipment which cover the chest and stomach areas.
dojo	道場	Club, place of training.
gasshuku	合宿	Training camp.
hakama	袴	A piece of clothing which covers the lower-body from waist down to the feet.
iaido	居合道	Martial art focussed on the drawing of the sword.
kata	形	Set forms practised as a way to learn the basic techniques of kendo.
keiko	稽古	The practice or training of budo (martial arts).
kendo	剣道	An athletic sport which is played by means of one-on-one striking between opponents using *shinai* and wearing *kendo-gu*.
kendo-gi	剣道着	A kimono-style top which is worn during *keiko* and matches.
kendoka	剣道家	A kendo practitioner.
kenshi	剣士	A kendo practitioner.
kote	小手	A piece of kendo equipment; the gloves which cover hands and forearms. One of the striking zones.
men	面	The piece of kendo equipment which covers the head, face, throat, and shoulders. One of the striking zones.
sensei	先生	Teacher or instructor.
senpai	先輩	One's senior.
shiai	試合	A match.

shihan	師範	A master; a person with exceptional character and kendo techniques who serves as an example. Also, a person in the position to teach kendo to students and disciples.
shinai	竹刀	A bamboo practice sword.
tsuki	突き	One of the striking/thrusting zones in kendo. A type of technique in which one thrusts at the opponent's throat.
taikai	大会	A gathering/meeting/tournament.

*The Kendo Terminology definitions were written with reference to the *Japanese-English Dictionary of Kendo* (2nd Ed., 2011) published by the All Japan Kendo Federation.

Hirokazu Okusa
Kendo Kyoshi 7-dan, Musoshinden-ryu Iaido 5-dan

Hiro was born in Nagano, Japan in 1946. His life-long kendo practice began as a 15-year-old at a high school in Tokyo. In 1974, when he was 28 years old, Hiro immigrated to Ontario, Canada and soon after joined Toka Budokan kendo club in Toronto. Upon his move to Vancouver in 1978, he attended the University of British Columbia (UBC), establishing its first kendo club during his studies. When he withdrew from UBC, he travelled with his *bogu* to Brazil, Argentina, and Chile. In 1989 he opened his own dojo, Zosokan, in a converted barn on his farm and enjoys teaching children and adults from the community. After teaching kendo at UBC for 27 years, he established the Simon Fraser University Kendo Club. From 2009–2014, Hiro was President of the Canadian Kendo Federation and a director of the International Kendo Federation. He is a retired landscaping developer, currently enjoying life as a hobby farmer. Hiro lives in Surrey, British Columbia with his wife, Noriko. He has three daughters and four beloved grandchildren. He can be contacted at okusa.hiro@gmail.com.

Hiro at Zosokan.

Printed in the USA
CPSIA information can be obtained
at www.ICGtesting.com
LVHW050901300923
759708LV00046B/1122